LITANY OF DEMENTIA: OR LIFE WITH ADRIAN

BY
SHARON SWAIN

TABLE OF CONTENTS:

DEDICATION

This book is dedicated to our two sons, who I have named as D___ and K___ to give them some anonymity. Like me they were on a learning curve concerning dementia, but when times were difficult they were there to support both Adrian and myself, and I would like to thank them both for their kindness and compassion.

COVER

The photograph used on the cover, was taken in the summer of 2013, and shows a happy moment, even though Adrian couldn't understand what was happening. Our son K___ was taking a photograph to send to his wife who was in the USA at the time. Adrian was asked to "wave to the camera", but couldn't understand the instruction. However, he was pleased to smile at me, because I was happy.

1. INTRODUCTION

Dementia is a journey that the sufferer, and their friends and loved ones, explore together. It can be a hard and tortuous path, with very little moments of relief along the way, and it may have to be endured by all concerned for many years. However, my experience says that the journey can be made easier, and there can be moments of respite and real happiness. All does not need to be doom and gloom from the moment the diagnosis is suspected. Although every person who suffers dementia will experience it differently, there are some simple actions that can often help the sufferer and their friends and family.

This is a book about the journey my husband Adrian and I took as he slowly lost his memory and as other signs of the disease began to show. It covers the first signs of his illness, to his eventual diagnosis of vascular dementia, his admission to a Nursing Home, and finally to his death. It also accompanies the journey that our family and friends made as we travelled with him, and as we learned to understand what was happening to him. It is not a diary, as I have tried to link occurrences together, and to allow others to see how we coped with the changes we experienced in my husband's day-to-day life.

For many people dementia is about memory loss, but dementia is much more than that as those who experience it understand. However, forgetfulness can be one of the first visible signs of the disease, although it can be caused by many other things. Sometimes it is part of growing older, or the result of infection or an underactive thyroid, or even Parkinson's disease. Each of these though will produce other effects upon the sufferer, and so does dementia.

This book only deals with memory loss from dementia and the effects upon my husband's life, and those around him. Since there are many different causes of dementia, how it showed its presence in Adrian's life might not therefore apply to everyone. However, many of us know more than one person suffering from dementia, and discussion about it seems to evoke memories of friends and loved ones who have suffered or who are suffering from this disease. As a non-medical person it seems to me that some of my experiences may well be shared by those who read this book, and hopefully the ways that I tried to mitigate the effects upon Adrian might also be useful to others.

For seven years I worked as a Religious Education Adviser and Children's Officer in a Church of England Diocese, and trained hundreds of teachers and church leaders in experiential education and worship. Experiential work seeks to use practical ways to uncover what people think and feel about themselves and about others. It helps them to learn to 'walk alongside others', and to explore their different lives. Games, role play, and craft activities are used to help adults and children to 'walk in the shoes' of someone else, and to engender compassion and understanding of the way others live their lives.

As my husband's memory loss became greater I began to wonder if I could use some of these techniques concerning experiential work with Adrian; could I began to apply the thinking behind the movement to my husband? I started by asking myself what it might feel like to live in such a fractured world, where nothing but the present and the extreme past exist; where those who spoke to me were often unknown to me; and where my mind was full of unanswered questions and worries.

After some false starts I managed to find ways of helping my husband that worked fairly well for us, although I needed to continue to change my methods as he moved into the later stages of dementia. The solutions were not perfect, and they may not work for you. I used what is referred to as the 'person centred' approach, which seeks to offer care that is tailored to an individual's personal needs and to their previous life experience. It is a way of helping to overcome or to ease behavioural problems as well as some of the psychological difficulties that sufferers can experience. The 'person centred' approach as the name suggests takes the individual seriously, giving them the respect and dignity they deserve, trying to work with them, taking note of their likes and dislikes, and finding ways of ensuring they can still have a rewarding and interesting life.

I learnt to be 'quick on the draw' when trying to find answers to problems, to skate round the truth if it would help Adrian, and to be imaginative and creative in my solutions. I also learnt to protect him at all costs – he was my sole concern for much of the time. I finally realised that it was no different to dealing with a young child who continually asks the question "Why?" all the time, and if Adrian didn't actually the question "Why?" out loud, I could see he was asking the question internally. Just as the answers had to keep coming and they had to be understood by the child, so with Adrian the solutions to difficulties needed to come fast and they had to make some sense to him at the time, even if five minutes later he had forgotten the whole situation.

I hope that you can make use of the ideas within this book about Adrian's journey into dementia, so that your journey in whatever capacity that is, might be made easier.

2. "MY WIFE HAS DIED"

Adrian, my lovely husband of 48 years effectively 'died' for me on 17th June 2013 when we both attended our local Surgery and he informed the Doctor in my presence that "his wife had died a few months ago".

"It's very sad" he said, the tears rolling down his face. "I miss her enormously".

I could not believe that my husband who never shared his emotional self with anyone was opening like a flower to the Doctor's gentle words. I sat just out of his sight feeling as if my world had collapsed around me despite already half-suspecting that he had forgotten who I was some time ago. Even as I listened in shock I remember being most impressed that the Doctor didn't even glance at me, but continued checking how Adrian was getting on 'without his wife'. He was sympathetic and gentle with him, as the imagined story came out of how he was managing alone. Finally the Doctor looked towards me.

"And who is this, then?" he asked, looking from one of us to the other.

Adrian turned my way, giving me the most beautiful smile and answered immediately, with no hesitation. "She's my Carer," he explained. "She's lovely!"

The word 'Carer' struck me as odd, even as I struggled to understand what was happening. It was a word I had never heard him use during the whole of our life together, and it felt alien to him. Perhaps, however, it was a word that he already realised was appropriate in his life. I had after all become his Primary Carer as the dementia bit deeper.

Before we left his room, the Doctor had made his preliminary diagnosis, of dementia. He explained that it could be any one of a number of different kinds of dementia. He talked to us about the Memory Clinic, held near the local Hospital in Haverfordwest, and began the process of arranging an appointment to attend. Finally he organised a CT scan of Adrian's head.

Leaving the Surgery a few moments later still in complete shock, I realised there was no point in discussing this with Adrian, unless he brought the subject up himself. I had already learnt that it was important to respond to events, or to answer questions, immediately. Five minutes later for someone with memory loss (and at this stage I could not use the word 'dementia') was simply too late! By now, I knew, that if I brought up the subject he might well respond that "of course I was his wife", and give me a puzzled look, totally confused as to what on earth I was talking about.

Adrian and I had been sent out from the Doctor's Surgery to start a new life, that of 'Dementia Sufferer' and 'Dementia Carer', with no idea of what the future held or how our lives would change. All we had was seemingly a death sentence for Adrian and for our mutual life together. However, I was to discover that this was not really the truth, there was life before dementia was diagnosed, and certainly afterwards. It was just a different kind of life!

3. THE BEGINNING OF MEMORY LOSS

Thinking back I had begun to realise there was a problem with my husband's memory some four years earlier although it had taken me a while to acknowledge there was any real difficulty. As we get older there are often times when we forget something as most mature people realise. It seems to be a part of the normal ageing process. Indeed I can remember driving down the M5 aged fifty years old, thinking about my boss and being unable to remember his job title. The harder I thought the more the word slipped silently away out of my mind. I had always found it difficult to remember names, although strangely Adrian had not. After this happened a few times I finally went to my Doctor, saying "I think I've got the beginnings of dementia!" Her response was to laugh, and inform me that I had started the menopause!

However, in 2009 I was beginning to realise that if I didn't have a problem, Adrian certainly did. Before this time we were apart for much of the week as I lived and worked in Cumbria (and for the six years prior to this, in Suffolk) and Adrian worked in Gloucester, returning throughout this time from his one-bedroom flat to the family home every Thursday. However, in 2008 Adrian had retired, and we were now together most of the time, although I was still working full-time.

The first major sign of Adrian having difficulties with his memory occurred when we bought ourselves a new caravan. We decided to take it away for a couple of days to familiarise ourselves with all the new controls and gadgets before going on our main holiday later that summer. There was nothing unusual about this, except that it was the first time we had used a more modern caravan. I was a little concerned whether we could manage to work out how to start the water heater, put on the lights, work the shower, and do all the many jobs needed to park the caravan when we arrived on the site. So it seemed like a good idea to have a trial-run of everything before going away later that year.

We had owned a number of caravans over the years, and Adrian was accustomed to hitching up the van, removing the brake and generally making all safe before leaving. He was also completely at home with setting up at a new site, so there should be no difficulties. I had always driven the family car and was happy to tow the caravan, particularly as Adrian was a good navigator. On holiday he would take great enjoyment in wickedly guiding me down impossible dead-end lanes that ended up at the sea with almost no turning point, so on one occasion we were actually forced to unhitch the small caravan and physically turn it round. On another occasion he navigated me into the middle of a village that was holding a festival in the Dales with hundreds of people present, and I was forced to do a three-point turn with the caravan. Alternatively though, he would get me circumventing large towns, like Liverpool, via a myriad of small country roads. This was of course in the days before the satnav existed.

Although Adrian had driven for years and owned his own car, he really preferred being a passenger. In the past he had always said that if he had to drive on a congested motor-way he would probably end up taking his hands off the wheel and scream. It was ironic that for twenty years he was to drive up and down motorways, doing thousands of miles to return to Suffolk and then later Cumbria. He never complained, and in fact said he enjoyed having the time in the car to de-stress after work. In later years he would also tell everyone mischievously that "I drove him to drink!" Actually he would usually walk to the pub or get a lift with friends, and I would then go and pick him up later! On one occasion I remember being stopped by the police who were doing some kind of check at midnight, to find a car full of slightly inebriated men driven by a woman with a dog-collar. They waved us on!

This particular weekend we had chosen a place to stay near Lockerbie, sufficiently far enough from home to be a good test for the new caravan, and yet near enough to get there after work that evening. Neither of us knew the area, which meant we could enjoy exploring over the next couple of days. The site was easy to find and the entrance was fairly wide. This was always my horror. Would I be able to negotiate the gate, had I chosen the right place, and if not would I be able to reverse out again? However, I managed to park the caravan into the correct place with no difficulty. The site was a little steep though and we needed help from another holiday-maker to get the caravan level. As we left to go and buy food though, I felt content that we could manage the new electrics.

When we returned it was getting dark, and there was still a lot of work to do. While I packed away the food, Adrian started preparing dinner. He was a good cook, and I had seen him produce a roast meal with Yorkshire puddings on a caravan stove, more times than I could remember. However, this night it was to be a quick and simple meal of sausage and mash.

"Where's the tin of beans?" Adrian asked.

"They're in the cupboard," I said, turning away to put some shoes under one of the seats.

There was silence – total silence! I looked round to find Adrian standing in the middle of the caravan looking perplexed. It was a shock to realise that he had absolutely no idea where the tins were, yet it had only been five minutes since I had put the food away, and showed him where I had stored them. Perhaps he'd not heard what I had said, I thought, after all his hearing was pretty bad. I showed him where I had put the packets and tins, and promptly put it out of my mind for the rest of the weekend.

In retrospect I was to realise what had happened, although it was some months before I could explain it to myself. Adrian had no recollection of where the food had been stored, so he needed to go back into his memory to find another example from the past and see if it worked. This was a new caravan – a strange new environment – and his internal pictures of our older caravans did not quite fit with the reality of the new caravan. For a start all the cupboards were in different places and there were many more of them. Where we had placed the food in the old caravan didn't quite match the reality now.

At the time I simply assumed he was tired, or hadn't heard me. He had travelled back from Gloucester to Cumbria that morning, before we finished getting ready to go away, and drove to Lockerbie. It was just a one-off incident I excused to myself, putting it out of my mind and enjoying the few days we had in Scotland.

But this was not to be a single incident, for on our summer holiday later that year Adrian forgot to take off the brake on the caravan and we were trailed by plumes of smoke until we stopped. I guess we had been about two minutes short of causing a fire the brake was so hot. However, once it cooled down the problem was fixed. After this I would surreptitiously check everything before we set off. I realised even then that he would be unhappy if he saw me following him around checking everything, so I didn't make a big deal of it. Already I was trying to 'put myself in Adrian's shoes' and covering up for him, something that families continually do for dementia sufferers I was to discover.

The next time I noticed any problem with Adrian's memory concerned our home computer. For the past twenty-eight years he had been a computer 'whizz-kid', having been trained to work on the RAF's main-frame computer. As a Systems Analyst he was accustomed to sorting out any problems, and I thought of him as a 'computer detective', able to fix anything that went wrong. For some years he had returned home to Worcester, or Suffolk, or Cumbria, indeed wherever we were living, on a Thursday morning. Then he would be on call to sort out the computer problems at work from wherever we lived. When the computer programmers were at a loss, they would turn to Adrian to sort out the computer itself. He was amazingly inventive at finding solutions, and indeed the computer firm had even head-hunted him back after he had left to take up a new job some years earlier. Every time they encountered a problem someone had said "You need Adrian", until finally they searched him out and offered him a job at a salary he couldn't refuse.

But if he could solve their difficulties he was also on hand when my home computer suffered any kind of glitch. I grew used to the fact that he was there to help me when I bought a new computer, or needed a new driver installing. Yet suddenly I noticed that he was unable to assist me, when for instance I had a problem printing from the computer. He just shrugged his shoulder and pulled a face indicating he didn't know what was wrong. Neither did he offer to try and fix the problem. In the end I was forced to ask one of our sons to assist me. I wasn't sure what to make of Adrian's attitude regarding the computer, since he was by nature someone who always helped, yet now he seemed unconcerned. In the mean-time though, despite this, things at home went on pretty much as before.

STARTING TO THINK OF SOLUTIONS

At Christmas that year we were lucky enough to have the help of a professional actor to direct the Church Nativity Play, which that year was being performed by some of the adults from the area. Adrian loved acting and took the part of John the Baptist's father, Zechariah. He had little to say, but quite a lot of action. After three or four rehearsals he seemed unable to remember his moves. He seemed to have no idea of where to go, and it was beginning to irritate others. I thought he was just playing up, which he had a habit of doing, particularly if I was involved in producing a play. He preferred to 'wing it' if he could, but this would always unnerve inexperienced actors. However, this time since he had virtually nothing to say, I was at a loss to know why he couldn't remember his moves.

I finally realised that he was having spatial difficulties, something that had affected him for much of his life. In solving the problem I discovered later that I was trying out the 'person-centred' approach. I was simply working on instinct. I realised if I was unobtrusively to help him, I needed to be pretty clever, because I didn't want to knock his confidence or his self-esteem. After some thought I was to solve the problem by ensuring that Elizabeth his 'wife' took him by the arm as though leaning on him. In reality she was guiding him around the stage, but he was encouraged to believe he was helping his 'wife' move around on the slightly uneven floor in case she had problems.

These events slowly went into my memory bank alongside other similar occurrences over the following weeks and months, until I was forced to acknowledge that something was definitely wrong with Adrian's memory. However, it was to take over three more years before dementia was actually diagnosed.

ADRIAN'S RETIREMENT

During the rest of the winter and early Spring I was very busy, and my health was none too good, but since Adrian had retired he was able to take some of the household chores from me in his usual generous fashion. He had worked until he was sixty-seven years old, but was now at home every day. Since I had always worked from home, Adrian was accustomed to my not being available when he was free. Our boys had grown up knowing that if I was in my study I was working, and if the door was shut I shouldn't be disturbed unless it was urgent.

The first year of Adrian's retirement had given us the time to adjust to being together every day, and despite some concern that we might need to work out a new way of being together, there were no difficulties. Adrian seemed to accept the long established rule of not disturbing me if the door was shut, especially if a meeting was being held. He grew very adept at offering refreshments and welcoming people, or helping put handouts together, before disappearing and finding something else to do. I loved having him around more, as well as not living alone in an empty house for half of the week now the boys had grown up and left. It was very good for me as I was forced to take time off and not work such long hours. I made sure that I finished early every afternoon and would stop to have a cup of tea with him, even if I had to do more work in the evening.

Adrian found new things to do in the daytime. Since we lived in a fairly isolated hamlet he would travel into the nearby small town to get his paper in the morning, then return to do the crossword before taking our two chocolate coloured Labrador dogs out for a walk. Then there was the shopping, the grass to cut, ironing to be done (like all servicemen he was very adept at this), and each evening he would cook dinner. Finally at the end of the day, a pint or two could then be had in a nearby village.

He seemed to enjoy the relaxed way of life, and not miss the stressful job of a Systems Analyst, or the long drive north each week. He settled in to the restful lifestyle in the midst of the Cumbrian countryside with a trip of four miles for a pint of milk or some bread, and seventeen miles to the nearest large town. We had always preferred living in a rural area, although in the early days of our marriage we had lived in Married Quarters, and then later moved from suburban estate to suburban estate. At a time when our teenage sons would have enjoyed the space of nearby fields and woods unfortunately we had lived on the edge of towns. Now when they had flown the nest my work had taken me to the empty spaces of a Suffolk estuary, followed by fifty-five square miles of the Cumbrian countryside.

During this first year of Adrian's retirement I changed my work-life balance on a daily and weekly basis to include more time with Adrian, and it was liberating for both of us. I had been working eighty-hour weeks up to this time. Now on a Thursday afternoon it became our habit to go to the coast just a few miles away, for a walk along the beach. We discovered a wonderful shop that sold ice cream all year round, and even on a bitterly cold day would call in for a cornet with one of their dozen flavours. Then we would let the dogs run free to chase the birds on the foreshore (which they never caught), or to run wildly into the sea. After an hour of trying to stop them from eating dead things, that sometimes included the fish caught on long lines laid along the beach at low tide, or stopping them from shaking their wet coats over us, we would return home feeling exhilarated and refreshed. For me this always signalled that my day off had arrived, and I would try to keep the evening free if possible.

At other times on a Friday we would go further afield to explore the Cumbrian fells or lakes, Adrian guiding me down obscure tracks to discover the lesser well known car-parks and foot-paths in the National Park. With the phone going continuously at home we found it therapeutic to get out, and to enjoy spending some time together. As well as bringing up our two boys we had at various times fostered a teenage girl, cared for elderly relatives and for many years we had both held down stressful jobs that took us to different parts of the country, consequently we were only together for extended weekends. This year showed us that a better lifestyle balance could be experienced, and I began to look forward to being retired myself, in two or three years.

THE MOVE TO PEMBROKESHIRE

That wish was to come true rather earlier than we thought, for I was unwell that Winter and Spring, and in the Summer of 2010 I took early retirement on health grounds. We would now need to move out of the Vicarage and find somewhere else to live. So we began the search for a new house. Wanting to be near the coast at first we started the search among the small towns along the west coast of Scotland. We began at Ayr, then moved south to Kirkcudbright, and finally along the Solway Firth opposite our present home. However, we could found nothing within our budget, and so gradually we continued moving south towards Liverpool. We had great hopes for a while of somewhere around Bolton le Sands, but that didn't work out. Avoiding the large towns we slowly entered Wales, passing Rhyl, Bangor, then into Ceredigion, and finally arrived at Pembrokeshire where like many people we had great memories of past holidays. However, we could find no house or bungalow that appealed to us, or was within our price range.

On the last day of our search, before going back to Cumbria for the last three months of our time there, we still hadn't found anywhere to live. It was getting scary! Then just as we were about to give up we discovered a bungalow near Pembroke that did our 'souls good'. By this I think we both meant somewhere with an outlook that looked over country rather than over other houses. The village had reasonable facilities and it was on a bus-route. A lot of work needed doing to the bungalow but we could see the potential. The garden looked over fairly wild and scrubby land but in the distance we could see farms and a long low hill. This was to be our first permanent home after the fifteen or sixteen moves that had occurred throughout our married life. The bungalow should suit us even if we lived into our eighties, for the village had both a shop and a pub, and it was on a bus route.

Adrian thought of our final move as 'coming home', for he had been born and brought up in Wales. Admittedly this was a different area, for he came from South Wales and the Rhondda, but with its largely English speaking population Pembrokeshire was a good substitute. It was also near the sea. Although we couldn't see it from the bungalow, the beach was only a mile away. Both of us had always wanted to live close to the sea, but never thought this would be possible.

Since our marriage in 1965 we had moved house every few years, and were accustomed to clearing out the junk, cleaning everything, and generally making sure the new place was ready for us to move into. After a life-time of travelling with the Army (in my case), the RAF (for both of us), and finally the Church, we were going to settle down permanently. Because the bungalow was smaller than our four-bedroomed Vicarage in Cumbria we were both determined to downsize our possessions. The last few months before the move were therefore very busy. During all this time Adrian seemed completely normal. I didn't notice anything strange in his behaviour or demeanour. He seemed much the same as usual.

Things went well with the move, and the plans we'd honed over many years went smoothly. We had become so accustomed to moving that we knew exactly what we had to do. Adrian was able to think back over forty years to earlier moves, and got on with the work, helping to pack boxes, taking the large furniture apart, dismantling the beds, and travelling to and from the local tip to dispose of the rubbish. Again he showed no loss of memory, and it was later I was to realise that this was probably because it was an activity he had been accustomed to carrying out from the first year of our marriage. He could return to an earlier memory to remind himself of what needed to be done, and as he came and went he was able to see the wardrobes or beds that hadn't been taken apart, and the bags of rubbish that were accumulating. Accordingly he would deal with them.

Adrian had always taken over the general handy-work associated with moving to a new house. He had never been a man who wanted to do serious DIY, but he was more than capable of installing the television, putting up flat-pack furniture, and ensuring the computer was on-line. He would also hang the pictures and put up any wall brackets that were needed. In the meantime I would unpack, and sort the kitchen and then all the other rooms, while Adrian travelled backwards and forwards to local towns to fetch anything that was needed, whether this was paint or a packet of screws. He would also do the weekly shop, for which I was for ever grateful.

As an ex-secretary, I had taken over the family administration many years before. Adrian might run the RAF's main-frame computer, but he had never liked doing any administration at home. It probably reminded him too much of work. So in the weeks before the move I sent out dozens of emails and letters with the details of our new address and our new phone number. I changed account details, dealt with new telephone and electricity providers, and organised the removal quotes. All of this work was to prove helpful in the years to come when Adrian was unable to contact any of these people himself anyway.

Our move this time was to be slightly different, because we had allowed ourselves space on the schedule to do work in the bungalow before actually moving. We had decided to get the electrics replaced, the bungalow painted, and new carpets fitted before we lived there. So before our move to Wales we spent a couple of weeks camping in the empty bungalow while all the work was done. The whole place was painted by our friend Mark who was a painter and decorator. He and his wife Jane (with whom I had worked some years earlier) and their son Andrew, spent some time in August with us sleeping in a tent in the garden. This was in fact the third house they had decorated for us – always in white. I had learnt that it was simpler to keep to one colour for at least our furnishings wouldn't clash with the colour.

During these couple of weeks before we actually moved in, Jane and Adrian went to the supermarket in Pembroke Dock to do some food shopping. She came back to say she had found it almost impossible to stop Adrian buying frozen food. He was determined to buy a normal week's shopping, despite the fact that we had no fridge or freezer in the bungalow because we hadn't moved in properly yet.

At this time we still had two cars, and Adrian would disappear to the nearest town to get anything that was needed. It usually meant a trip to the supermarket as well as the local hardware store. For years Adrian had done the food shopping early on a Saturday morning. He enjoyed getting outside after working in a building with no windows and only artificial light all week. He would stroll up and down every aisle, rather than go specifically to a certain place to find an item. In retrospect I realised that he didn't remember where any article could be found, but simply searched the entire supermarket checking if there was anything he thought might be needed. The result was his shopping could be somewhat eclectic, and we often ended up throwing away a lot of food. It also took him a long time to do the shopping each week, and things were always forgotten, necessitating more trips to the supermarket.

The first sign of any major problem with Adrian occurred while the bungalow was being painted. One morning he left to go and get some decorating materials from Pembroke Dock which was about nine miles away. However after three hours had gone by we were still waiting for the paint, so I rang his mobile. There followed a long rather garbled tale of shopping queues and traffic jams, all of which sounded very odd. He seemed to be in the supermarket car-park, though I wasn't sure if he had actually bought the paint, or if he was about to return home.

There was clearly something wrong, but over the phone I couldn't really discover what it was. Taking a deep breath I decided it was easier to collude with his story at this stage, rather than get into an argument over the phone. His hearing was bad and he never wore his hearing aid, so it seemed unlikely he would hear everything I was saying. I suggested he stayed where he was, making the excuse that I wanted his help in choosing some curtains and I would join him shortly.

This simple decision was to be one of the most important decisions I made in the early days of our joint dementia journey, and it was to set a pattern for our lives in the future. I had realised instinctively that it wouldn't help to question Adrian, for we would only end up having a disagreement at a distance, which would hardly be satisfactory for either of us. I noted that he sounded fairly stressed over the phone, and knew that questioning him at this point would only make things worse. It seemed more important simply to rescue him. Even at this early stage I realised that I was actually doing just that – going to the rescue! I wanted to remove the problem and protect him. It was what I had done for our two boys when they were small giving them a hug to make everything better, even if that didn't always work. I applied the same thing to Adrian metaphorically, and his worried voice just felt like a siren call. I needed to be with him. I knew I could discover the actual problem later in the day.

In the event I didn't discover what had happened that day. Adrian had done all the shopping and was in the supermarket car-park when I arrived. We continued to look at curtains, and returned home later that afternoon. Mark's work on the walls was a little delayed, but I brought back a contented Adrian who by now didn't appreciate that there had been any problem, but was happy that I was with him.

4. DRIVING AND CARS

In fact it was to be another week before I actually learned the cause of the difficulty that Adrian had experienced that morning in the supermarket car park. I made the discovery through my friend Jane's son, Andrew, when he travelled with Adrian to the supermarket the following week. It turned out that he had been unable to find his way home! To be fair, I didn't find it that easy at first either, and would get confused by the different roundabouts, and whether I should travel down this A road or that A road – there being at least two ways in which we could return home. Adrian was able to find his way to Pembroke Dock, because of the signposts, but couldn't find his way back to where we lived because there were no signposts to our village until about a mile away from home. He had never had any sense of direction, so I wasn't surprised.

In those early days I assumed that Adrian's inability to find his way round his new environment was simply Adrian at his best! The boys and I were accustomed to him losing his way in a department store or in a town, or else in the woods when we were out walking. Sometimes he would be standing beside us one moment, and then gone the next. He had never had any sense of direction, and frequently just wandered away, or would argue "We need to take this path to get out of the forest", when I and our sons knew categorically he was wrong. Indeed during his career in the RAF he had been forbidden to attend parades, because he couldn't tell his right hand from his left, and as youngsters our lads learnt to watch out for him, rather than the other way around. He would simply cross the road when it suited him, leaving the boys on the opposite side of the road about to step into the path of ongoing traffic because they had been too slow to follow him.

In the coming month though it was quickly borne in upon me that something else was wrong. This was not just his failure concerning his sense of direction. Usually after a few abortive attempts he would find our new home, but this time although he found the shops he seemed totally unable to return home. After Andrew informed his mother "I'm never going in the car with Adrian again!" I also realised I had to persuade Adrian to give up driving. He was obviously unable to cope with the road system around us, and was becoming a danger to himself and to everyone else. He had always laughed an elderly aunt who had lived with us, after she went over a mini roundabout and said, "Who put that strange thing there?" But now he was proving to be equally dangerous to other road-users.

All this occurred years before Adrian's dementia was diagnosed, and sometimes I felt as though I were tiptoeing on glass if I wasn't to upset him. I constantly needed to consider long and hard how I handled him. It was like dealing with a recalcitrant toddler, and this thought occurred to me more than once in the future as his dementia increased. If I needed a good outcome then I had to proceed cautiously. Over the coming months and years I began trying out various strategies using my knowledge of 'walking in someone else's shoes', and asking myself questions like "How might Adrian feel?" After he was diagnosed with dementia I finally read about different philosophies on how to work with sufferers, sometimes trying the new ideas out, and usually wishing I had known about them earlier.

However, at this time I was still coming to terms with the fact that his memory seemed to be failing. Indeed I had not even acknowledged to myself that Adrian had dementia. He was only five years older than I and in his sixty-ninth year at the time. I knew little about the disease and if I did think about it, I wouldn't have believed that a man of his age with such an intelligent brain could be suffering from dementia. At this time it was the practical things that engaged me and the question of how to persuade him to give up driving concerned me considerably during that summer.

GETTING RID OF THE CAR

For most men their car is their seat of power, connected in some mysterious way to their sense of identity. This was not quite so with Adrian, but his car did give him freedom, so that although he had retired he was not reliant on me. If I was at a conference or meeting he was able to go out, or if I wanted to go early to some event then he could travel later. It suited us to have two cars, but if he were to give up driving, then I would need to make sure that we sold one of the cars as well. It would be a double blow, I thought.

We had a good marriage, one that had always been a little different to many, especially in the nineteen sixties and seventies. I had gone back into full-time education the year after we returned to England from our first posting abroad, and then travelled from Norfolk to Sussex University each week for two years. For three years after this Adrian had then travelled from his posting in Northern Ireland to Sussex every couple of weeks. The Government had a small majority, and he was able as a member of the RAF to hitch a ride in the airplane that returned the Minister of State for Northern Ireland to England, when there was an urgent need for the latter to vote. When I first went off to university many people thought that our marriage had broken up, but in fact these separations made it stronger.

Adrian took over most of the housework, even though it was long before any kind of equality in the home. Most men would not have been seen doing such a thing at this time, they wouldn't hang out the washing or push a pram. It was still a time when men expected their meal to be on the table when they returned home after work. But Adrian had no such qualms about going against the grain. He was a man who was confident in himself, and in his abilities. Despite having no formal academic qualifications he was an extremely clever man. My burgeoning academic career proved to be no problem to him in fact he was always proud of my achievements.

But the question now was would his self-esteem stand my saying, "That's it! You're not driving anymore!" followed by an ultimatum that said, "I'm selling your car!" After all we hadn't even talked about his memory problems yet, and I wasn't sure if he knew that he had a problem. He had never spoken of any concern. It was just possible that while trying to find his way home at least a dozen times, he might still have thought this was his usual problem when negotiating a new area.

Adrian had never been in the habit of talking about his thoughts, and it was sometimes impossible to know what he felt about any changes in his life. He was a man who looked backwards rather than forwards. He would meet someone accidently (for instance while passing through the centre of London), someone that he had known fifty years before, and he would recognise them instantly and know their name. On the other hand he would wake up on the first day of a holiday not having thought about it all. I could never get him to decide what clothes he wanted to take with him, or even where we were to stay. It wasn't long before I realised I needed to do all the planning and make sure things like holidays actually happened.

Another example of this inability to look ahead and prepare, occurred early in our marriage. For three or four years he talked about doing some academic study. He had left school at fifteen with no qualifications, and then gone into the RAF fairly young. Now the thought of getting some examinations began to appeal to him. I offered to work to put him through college when he left the RAF. As an experienced PA I was sure I could get a good job, which together with the grants that were being offered at that time, would have kept us viable financially. Adrian seemed interested. However, I noticed that this idea never actually materialised, nothing ever happened to turn the idea into reality. He didn't join classes run by the Education Officer to get his O levels for example, or go to the local College and join an evening class. I concluded after a while that it was all talk, and that it wouldn't happen. He was not sufficiently motivated. Consequently, I began to look at going to College myself, and while we were in Cyprus I took some O level exams. It was interesting that eventually many years later Adrian did actually take a couple of exams, and ended up teaching O level Mathematics to airmen on the camp where he was stationed. But he never took this any further. For me, as someone who planned their life (allowing for different outcomes), and who always had a vision of how the future might be, this inability to look ahead drove me mad in the early days.

Perhaps the worst example of Adrian's lack of concern over the future though occurred many years later when our first son D___ was born. During the months of my pregnancy I happily planned the whole scene from the baby's bedroom – choosing the paint for the walls, and making the curtains – to the clothes he or she would wear. My mind was full of possibilities. However, I couldn't get Adrian to even think about what our life might be like with a baby around, especially what difficulties there might be after being childless for thirteen years. He seemed uninterested in talking about the future, or in buying anything for the baby, and if given his way would have woken up on the first day of the child's life with nothing in place at all. In fact right up to the night of our son's birth this was so, yet the morning after the birth Adrian was at the shops buying dozens of clothes and toys. He could deal with the reality of a situation, and he could look back into the past, but he could never plan ahead or visualize the future.

Anyway on the subject of driving, despite all I have said, Adrian must actually have done some thinking about what might happen if he didn't stop driving. Perhaps the situation of getting totally lost had shocked him, for when I finally plucked up the courage to open the conversation a day or so after our friends had left, to my amazement he met me more than half way.

I decided to attack the problem laterally. I wouldn't suggest he stop driving, instead I would tackle the issue of having two cars. Then later I could deal with his driving.

"It might be a good idea to get rid of one of the cars," I said casually one morning, when we were both in the kitchen. "We really don't need two cars now we've got bus passes!" I fought hard with myself not to turn this into a question, but to offer it to him as a statement. Questions caused problems sometimes, as he sought to try to find an answer but couldn't find one. But how difficult it was not to ask a question, I thought.

There was silence for a moment, as Adrian finished cooking bacon that Saturday morning. It appeared that he wasn't going to speak.

In the end I could bear the silence no longer and I had to give in and ask a question. "What do you think?"

"Perhaps you're right." He passed me a bacon sandwich on a plate, and then said no more.

I picked up the conversation again a few minutes later, over our late breakfast. "Now we're not working, and you're not travelling halfway across the country, we can enjoy each other's company in one car!" I did mange not to say "Can't we?"

Adrian glanced up from his food, and looked at me thoughtfully. He didn't appear to find the subject difficult to talk about and neither did it seem to upset him. "We could sell mine. It's a smaller car than yours, and it's done a lot of mileage," he said. With that he went on eating his breakfast and the conversation seemed to be closed. He was content that we had made a decision.

Presumably I just had to get on and try to sell the car. I did a mental high-five. The first step had been achieved, and the next should be easier. Adrian had always liked being a passenger and when we travelled together I always drove. I had passed my test a good many years before him, and he had always said that he really didn't want to drive. It was only when my job moved me to the other side of Gloucester that we had to face the reality of how he was to get to and from work. In the early days he rode a scooter, but later when we moved to Worcester he bought himself a car. It took him quite a few attempts to pass his test, but he finally did, and I think he enjoyed as I said earlier, the fact that the journey gave him time to wind down after a hectic day at work.

STOPPING DRIVING

We achieved the sale of his car, which left us with the larger family car that had been mine. Adrian could obviously drive this when he wished, and I now needed to think through the second phase of the plan. How was I to stop him driving? I cared too much for him to put him in danger, or for that matter to see others put in danger. But neither did I want to be heavy handed about this and remove his driving licence, so I needed to find another way. This required some ingenuity on my part, for there would be times he would want to drive the car, perhaps when I was out but not using the car, or if I was otherwise occupied in the house. When we went out together he took it for granted that I would drive. He was a good navigator and I enjoyed listening to him giving me directions from an OS map, usually finding the most interesting routes.

I decided the only thing to do was to remove one set of car keys and for these to go conveniently 'missing'. The second set of keys could be kept with me wherever I went. Hopefully Adrian would not find this suspicious. Secondly I needed to make sure that if he wanted to go anywhere I should be free to take him, even if this meant him waiting for a little while. At this stage he didn't forget things immediately but would be content to wait if I gave him a cup of coffee or tea, or suggested he watch television for a little, and if I said I would be ready to go out shortly. Over the coming weeks I tried this out and it worked a treat. It seemed as though there would be no need to send his driving licence back to the DVLA.

During this time I definitely began to realise that I needed to be a good planner. I must also be capable of adapting any plan at the drop of a hat should the situation change. I concluded, with a somewhat wry smile, that I needed to be distinctly devious and able to tell white lies should the need arise. I consoled myself with the thought that I was doing it for Adrian's good, to keep him and those around him safe, and happy. I was beginning to recognise the awful blank look of incomprehension when he was faced with a situation or a question that he didn't understand, and I would do almost anything to help him return to the peaceful place in his mind that he inhabited most of the time.

5. BANKING AND TAX AFFAIRS

THE DIFFICULTIES OF COPING WITH A BANK ACCOUNT

On my mind in 2010-11 were also some other rather large issues that needed solving. One concerned our banking methods. Adrian had an account with a Bank in Northern Ireland. This was originally opened when he had been stationed there for three years so that his wages could be paid into a local bank. Somehow it had never changed, and now his pensions were paid into this joint account. Initially this had not mattered, but over the years the bank had been taken over twice by different companies unknown to either of us. Adrian had found the staff at the local branch in Northern Ireland very warm and welcoming, always willing to deal with his questions and spend time talking to him, so he had never felt the need to change the account. However, when online banking was introduced we discovered a problem.

Adrian's deafness (and his dislike of his hearing aid) caused the first difficulty. He was unable by this time to hear most people on the phone, and was forced to ask me to intervene. This was certainly necessary every time he rang the bank. Unfortunately the staff at the branch seemed to find it impossible to understand the simple request, "Would you deal with my wife?" They really only wanted to speak to Adrian. If he asked them to speak to me he still had to answer certain questions about his account before they would deal with me, and not being able to hear them created something of an impasse. When the branch no longer answered the telephone because all the small branches had been centralised the difficulties grew even worse. Now there was no-one who knew him or who recognised his voice.

As his memory loss grew worse I began to dread ringing the bank. In February of 2011 Adrian returned from Tenby having gone there on the bus to say that he had lost his bank card. We re-traced his footsteps but were still unable to find it, and finally he was forced to ring up the bank and cancel the card. The resulting telephone conversation made me feel very uneasy, as though they thought I was trying to steal his money, despite the fact we were talking about our joint account. This was my first experience of a bank only wanting to deal with the first name on the account.

"My husband would like you to talk to me as he is deaf and cannot hear over the phone," I said, taking the phone from Adrian.

"Can I please speak to Mr Swain?" returned the anonymous voice as they followed their procedures to check that he wasn't being coerced to give away his bank details.

Then followed five minutes of conversation which Adrian couldn't hear, and if he could hear he couldn't understand. I intervened, with the same result they must speak to Adrian first. This continued for another five minutes as the bank clerk had by now completely forgotten he was supposed to speak to me. I was unsure by this time who was finding it more difficult to cope, the bank, me, or Adrian!

In the same month Adrian struggled to use the small digital card to handle his account on line, and I was forced to ring the Northern Ireland bank again, finally getting them to speak to me after about half-an-hour. (I dreaded to think what the telephone cost would be!)

"The card needs to be reset every time wrong numbers are pressed," I was informed. "Just pop into the branch, and we can reset it for you," said the lovely Irish voice.

"But we're in Wales," I pointed out.

There was no answer to this.

The "Can you speak to my wife?" instruction grew exceedingly tedious over the next few months, and it became obvious that I would need to do something much more drastic very soon. If Adrian couldn't handle his financial affairs, even with my help, it might mean that his money would be locked up and unobtainable, unless they were prepared to deal directly with me. Thinking about this some years later I realised I should have put the telephone on 'speaker phone' so that we could both have communicated with the bank clerk together. It didn't occur to me at the time, and in retrospect I'm not sure if the phone had that facility.

So finally I began to give serious consideration as to how I could persuade Adrian to move this joint account to England and to another bank. It did help that he had allowed me to complete his Tax Form that year after I had caught him struggling to fill it in. I showed him how I filled in my form by creating a photocopy first, which I then filled in using a pencil, before copying the figures onto the actual form. He was content to let me do the same for him, before he signed the finished document.

SOLUTION:- NOT TO ASK QUESTIONS, BUT BE CREATIVE

I was still struggling at this time not to ask Adrian questions, which made the whole subject of dealing with the bank account even more difficult. Asking questions would often just elicit a blank look. Unless he could match my question with an incident from his past that made some sense, he was unable to answer me, and I would get a blank stare or a puzzled look. He was also beginning to take in less new information all the time. He seemed unable to remember fresh facts, or anything that happened recently, and so most questions unless they were about the past made absolutely no sense to him.

It finally came to me that I could perhaps show Adrian how easy banking could be locally. Demonstration and creativity could sometimes get through to him where a carefully crafted argument didn't work. Perhaps if we could physically enter a bank and speak to the staff; if I could show him how easy it was for me to handle my own personal bank account, then possibly I could persuade him to move our joint account to Pembrokeshire.

So on a journey into Pembroke just after a difficult conversation with the bank in Ireland I dropped into my branch – a different bank – to ask a couple of questions about my account and to put in a cheque. The counter staff greeted me with a smile, and spoke to me by name. I introduced them to Adrian, and after I had finished we left to walk down the High Street.

"It might be nice to be able to drop into your bank," I said casually, almost keeping my fingers crossed behind my back.

"Yes," he said quite naturally. "I used to do that in Downmarket when I was stationed in Ireland."

"Pity we can't do that now. Ireland's too far away," I commented.

"I don't know any of them now, anyway," he said.

"No, well I expect young Bank Clerks move on to other jobs fairly quickly."

There was a pause before he responded. "Perhaps we could move my account to Wales."

"I could open a joint account for us here," I offered, keeping my voice matter of fact.

"Good idea!" he said finally.

There was no eye contact, no enthusiasm, just an acceptance that this might be a good possibility. Indeed I was unsure if he forgot the whole conversation shortly afterwards, but I took his words to be agreement to the plan, and periodically reminded him of the decision.

In the coming week we went into the branch again and opened a joint account. I wrote a letter to the Irish bank which we both signed and closed the old account. Finally I arranged for his pensions to be paid into the new joint account. Adrian was happy that he had his own bank card, and content that I would handle the payment of our bills. I kept my own personal account, realising that to have two separate accounts would be a good idea in case bank cards went missing, or Adrian depleted all the money in our joint account. To this end I also made sure my own account was sufficiently healthy at all times. I had to be open to all possibilities if I was to protect us both in the future.

In the years to come the decision to have a joint bank account connected to a branch nearby was another of those important decisions that was to make the future easier on a day to day basis. It was also easier eventually to sort out affairs upon his death, and took five minutes to transfer the joint account into my name when I took in his death certificate. I have never seen bureaucracy work so quickly and efficiently.

However money was to be a concern for Adrian through to the end of his life, although I found it difficult to discover the cause of his worry at the time. Like many people with dementia he felt that someone had "taken his money" and this subject would reappear periodically. He would never speak to me about this, and since he didn't know I was his wife for some years, he must have thought I had taken his money. Instead he would suddenly say to a friend or Carer, "They've taken my money!"

I learnt not to take this personally, for we had always shared all our money. A rational Adrian would never have even questioned this. After forty-seven-plus years of marriage what was mine was his, and what was his was mine! Indeed his generous spirit would cheerfully have given away everything he had. But an Adrian with memory-loss could not make sense of what was happening.

Occasionally, I would find an appropriate moment to bring up the subject of "They've taken my money", and point out that he had a wallet with cash in it, and a bank card. I encouraged him to spend some of his money when we were out, so that he would pay for a coffee, or buy things from the local shop. He had always drawn out cash from an ATM when doing the food shopping, and he was able to do this for a long time. Initially I would hover along-side him to check that he put in the correct numbers, and then in later years I would put the numbers in myself, with him standing beside me. He would then take the money and put it into his wallet.

As his memory diminished, so did his knowledge about finance, so that finally he was no longer able to handle money at all. He didn't understand what coins he was handling, and the cost of items he wished to buy. I kept him 'in the loop' for as long as possible, even if it meant that I had to give him the money to pay for something, and then allow him to retain the change. I discovered it was exactly like teaching a small child to handle money – give them money, help them to spend it, and encourage them to put the change in their wallet or purse. During this time he was liable to give our sons a twenty pound note "for a pint", which was fine, but he would do this to the same son two or three times in an evening. They were forced to find ways of putting the money back into his wallet or use it to buy him drinks.

At other times he would sit fingering the coins by the side of his bed where he had always put his money overnight, and in the end quantity became more important than the actual amount. So if there were twenty coins he would consider this to be quite a lot of money. Finally I would put spare foreign holiday money into his wallet and this would content him as he had lost the ability to actually spend it. My ultimate concern always had to be what would keep Adrian content; what would stop that anguished look that would appear on his face when he could not make sense of something.

ACHIEVING POWER OF ATTORNEY

By 2013 with Adrian's memory failing there was one other important official thing that needed to occur, before it became too late. I needed to get Lasting Power of Attorney for Adrian in order to be able to deal with all of his affairs in the future. There was a need to get this before his understanding grew too limited. As it turned out it was only just made in time. Another three months would have been far too late. By now I was dealing with all his affairs behind the scenes, but if he had to deal officially face to face with the tax people or his pension provider without any assistance from me, then more than this would be needed. Getting Lasting Power of Attorney felt like an enormous hurdle, but in the event the whole process went very smoothly.

I explained to Adrian that I needed to have his permission to deal with his pension authorities, the bank, and the tax people on his behalf. This would mean that he would not have to speak to them over the phone. He would still have his money (that is, his wallet with money in it and his bank card), but he would not have to be bothered to fill in his tax form for instance. He could still open his bank statements (in fact he had never done this, or if he had, he had never checked them when they arrived in the post) and he could put them in the filing cabinet. I also explained that in order for us to get Lasting Power of Attorney he would need to appoint two people to make sure that all was safe and that no-one was taking anything from him. The first person was someone who should be told when the Lasting Power of Attorney was being registered and they acted rather like an Executor. In fact he could nominate up to five people to ensure that all was being fairly handled on his behalf, but it was decided only to use one. He suggested that our son K___ could be this person, because our elder son D___ might not always be in this country. The second person to be appointed was called 'A Certificate Provider', and their job was to ensure that Adrian understood the authority he was giving me. They were also to check that I was not pressurising him. We both felt that a neighbour fulfilled this role perfectly.

I went onto the Government's website, downloaded the forms, and began to fill them in. I found this stage of the process extremely easy even though I'm not particularly computer literate, and the information that accompanied the form was also easy to understand. The cost for the whole process was very reasonable.

I explained to our neighbour what was needed and he came and talked with Adrian without me being involved in the conversation. At the end he asked if Adrian was happy with all the arrangements, and my husband agreed to go ahead and sign the forms. Our signatures were then witnessed by the neighbour.

My conversation over the whole subject took place over a few weeks, did not involve questions, and I did not push Adrian into a corner but tried to let him think through the whole subject as much as he could on his own. I did not want to emphasise his lack of ability to cope with financial affairs for it would surely depress him, but I did want him to look at the reality of the situation if he could. For the fact was that if he couldn't deal with the pension and tax people on his own, then these people would not be prepared to talk to me without his permission. That authorisation could only occur while he understood what was being asked of him, and I realised that might only last for a few more months.

Following the instructions on the Government website I subsequently sent K___ his part of the agreement, and registered the relevant forms with the authorities. The Power of Attorney came in to operation soon afterwards. In actual fact it made little difference to what had been happening, but it did give me the assurance that if Adrian became worse I would have permission to deal with the various authorities. I subsequently registered the Lasting Power of Attorney with the Bank, the Building Society and the Tax Authority. I finally went to register this with an old bank which he had used in the past. Apparently there were a few pounds left in the account. While they were photocopying the front page, they accidentally left it on the machine. It was to cause me problems, because I needed to get another copy from the relevant authority. Moral - always check what is left on a photo-copier!

In retrospect we should have appointed an extra person to have Power of Attorney, for it occurred to K___ and I after Adrian had gone into the Nursing Home that should I die before Adrian there would be a problem. If that happened then there could have been a scenario where the bungalow would have remained empty until his death, with no-one to oversee it, since our wills left our assets to each other, and only after the second death to our sons. In the event this was not to happen, but perhaps we should have thought about it earlier, for it would have saved some considerable worry at the time.

At the time I decided not to register for Power of Attorney concerning Adrian's health. I knew his wishes concerning resuscitation, for we had discussed them a number of times in the past, and the cost of adding this to the package seemed unnecessary. In the event, years later when he entered the Nursing Home, the Doctor's Surgery was changed to one nearer to the Nursing Home, and my wishes concerning his 'end of life' were then registered.

6. LEARNING TO COPE WITH CHANGES

In the first few years of Adrian's memory loss I coped with any difficulties on an *ad hoc* basis as they arose. Many of these situations were made easier because he was basically a kind and gentle man, treating others with respect. It was part of his nature to open doors for people, and to cook a meal that each person would enjoy even if this meant creating four separate meals. His love for children and dogs was legendary, and he was described by many as a 'true gentleman'.

LEARNING TO HAVE PATIENCE

Many dementia patients become angry and even violent quite early on during their illness as their intellect deteriorates, but Adrian largely remained his normal gentle self, although there were to be one or two exceptions to this in the last few years of his life, all connected to aspects of personal hygiene.

Almost the whole of his working life had been with the Royal Air Force, first as a member of the RAF and then later working for a private company at the same job, as a Systems Analyst. An extremely clever man, I had never heard him swear (well he had shouted "bunny-rabbits" after dropping a heavy metal drawer of cutlery on his foot once, which sent those of us present into giggles for half-an-hour) and he rarely if ever lost his cool. He could certainly get very insistent on his viewpoint, and could be prejudiced about certain things and certain people. However, perhaps because of his normally equable temperament I was able to make changes to our life long before his dementia was officially recognised, without too many difficulties. Having said this, he did sometimes forget what had been decided and try to revert to something agreed in the past.

Despite his fairly peaceful temperament I learnt very quickly at this time that if I wanted to keep Adrian happy then I needed to keep my cool with him. It did not help if I lost my patience with him, because he would become confused. This was easier said than done for I was born with a quick temper. However if any of us snapped at him or were short tempered with him it simply made his thinking more muddled. This also applied to disagreeing with him. Disagreements would pull him up short, and he would start to question everything he knew and could quickly become depressed.

All of this was sometimes very difficult, but I did manage to keep my patience with him most of the time. I put this down to coping with my mother and an aunt many years earlier. My mother lived with us for some time after having a serious stroke. I was not very patient with her (I could snap at her and sometimes I found myself screaming inside my head at her), but I was infinitely better with my aunt of ninety -odd years who came to live with us a few years later. Now faced with a husband who needed my total patience, I got my act together! I can remember being very grateful to my mother and aunt for teaching me how to care compassionately for someone.

Still it wasn't all plain sailing. There was the first year that he forgot my birthday. He had forgotten our wedding anniversary four days before this, but that was pretty normal. We had never made much of our anniversary. However, he had never forgotten my birthday. It had been an easy date to remember for someone in the RAF, for it was on Battle of Britain Day, and he had always made it a very special day. I think it had been he who reminded our boys in the past. This year though, he had forgotten. The odd thing was that he didn't seem to think there was anything special about a birthday. It was as though he didn't know people celebrated such things. So it felt very peculiar when I told him he had missed my birthday, and he didn't apologise. For Adrian that was very out of character for he thought about other people all the time. I remember thinking that one of us would need to remind him of birthdays in future!

THINKING ON MY FEET, AND NOT DISAGREEING

In these early months of his memory loss I sometimes had to deal with some peculiar suggestions from Adrian. In the autumn he suddenly decided it would be a good idea to go back to work because it would give us some more money, not that we needed any more income! He pointed out that he had been offered an extended contract for another two years, but had refused it because it meant going to work in the East of England. Now nearly three years after his retirement and almost seventy years old, he thought he should take up this job opportunity!

Following my principle of not disagreeing with him, because this caused him to be very stubborn as well as confused, I needed to find another way of handling Adrian at this point. It was no good my saying "What a stupid idea," which was my first reaction. That would not help at all. I quickly racked my brain for a solution. I had noticed that although he forgot facts, he was less likely to forget emotions, and I wondered if I could use this to help handle such a possibly difficult situation. I needed to defuse the situation fast.

"That sounds like a good idea but let's get our holiday out of the way first!" This was the first thing I could think of, that might distract him and yet cheer him up.

His face lightened, and he smiled at the thought of a holiday. A few moments later he was happily looking at the holiday brochures that we had collected a few days previously. The job, a fact, was forgotten, but the happy emotions connected to having a holiday kept him going for some-time that day. The job was hardly mentioned again.

Sometimes simple solutions did not quickly occur to me, and at other times I was unable to be as conciliatory. However, I was learning all the time the art of the possible and the impossible – what worked and what didn't work. My sole concern was to care for Adrian, try to keep him safe, and to protect our way of life. I had barely recognised that his memory loss was caused by dementia at this time. In retrospect I think I was probably in denial.

CHOICES AND STATEMENTS

Over the years the family and I learnt to collude with Adrian's assessment of any difficulties that he was having, and help him to keep his sense of self-worth. We soon stopped making excuses for him as we observed the changes that were occurring in his life, and instead started to find ways of helping him come to terms with what was happening. The need to never question Adrian took some achieving, and there were often times when we didn't manage to succeed. It was a case of trying to get it right the next time, and because Adrian didn't remember many of the times we got it wrong, we were able to do this. Gradually we learnt to use statements as opposed to questions, and to offer choices. The phrases "We could" or "I could" became great friends.

Early one morning Adrian and I had talked about going out with the dogs that afternoon. But after lunch he had forgotten this plan, so I needed to initiate the conversation once more. How I set about this would end up being important for our future life together, although I didn't realise it at the time.

I didn't want to remind Adrian that he had forgotten the conversation of that morning. So there had to be another way. I decided to make a suggestion to him, as though I had just thought of it, and as though I was going out on my own. He was always happy to follow my lead in this way, and he didn't need to worry that he might have forgotten something, which inevitably led on to a question about why he had forgotten our discussion of that morning. All of which led him into a downward spiral.

"I think I'll take the dogs for a walk," I said on this particular bright but chilly afternoon.

"Oh good idea, I'll come with you!" he said suddenly, looking up.

Another issue that immediately raised its head concerned the dog's leads. I was aware that both leads seemed to be missing and there was no point in asking

Adrian what he had done with them after returning from the shop that morning. I needed to use my imagination as to where they might be, and try to get his help to find them.

"Hang on a second I need to find their leads," I continued, lying through my teeth. "I must have put them somewhere when I came indoors."

He tutted at my seeming mistake but was immediately motivated at the thought of a walk down to the beach to help find the leads, which he thought I had mislaid. In the meantime I began to think of what he might have done with them. The kitchen was my first port-of-call, but there was no sign of them. Were they in the conservatory; or the garage? Any of these places might have been where he had released the dogs on his return. There was no point in asking him because Adrian wouldn't remember, but at least he was looking in different places to see if he could find them.

The leads were subsequently discovered hanging alongside his jacket in the conservatory. I left with a happy Adrian, trouble averted. He assumed that I had left them there the last time I returned home, as my coat (as well as his), hung alongside them. So he had no need to try and work out why he had forgotten the leads, or to be reminded of how difficult things were for him. Subsequently we had a pleasant afternoon walking the dogs on the beach.

I had learnt it was politic if I took the blame, so that he could be reassured that he wasn't at fault. This gave him peace of mind, and meant that he could stop questioning what was wrong with him, and why he couldn't make sense of his world. A contented Adrian was a thing definitely to be wished.

GIVING PHYSICAL CLUES

Some activities in our life had to be changed to help Adrian, and all of this happened long before he was diagnosed with dementia. One such part of our life that I needed to consider concerned my work as a parish priest. Although I had retired I still helped out in the parish and diocese. One of the jobs involved interviewing those who thought they had a calling to become a priest. Some of these people I would see once a month, or every six weeks, for up to two years as I tested their vocation. These were strangers coming into the house, who would join me in my study, where the door was then shut. This meant that Adrian was separated from me for an hour, and normally left on his own in the house.

In the early days of his memory loss, in the first year of his retirement, Adrian would offer to make a pot of tea or coffee for visitors as they arrived. He had been accustomed to doing this for many years, and I valued it enormously. During my ministry I might be faced with distraught parishioners, and there was nothing like a cup of tea or coffee to help with the discussion. So he knew that these visitors would appreciate a drink.

Over the years, however, I needed to change the routine a little as Adrian's powers diminished. Firstly I could not leave him to make the tea or coffee on his own, so I was forced to adapt that plan as the months went by. I tried various things and the most simple thing that worked and didn't make Adrian question my actions, was to lay a tray out ahead of the visit, and then to take it into the study. This just left him to boil the kettle and pour it into the teapot. He was able to do this for a year until I had to adapt the plan again. Finally I involved those coming to see me to help with Adrian. He would open the door for them and welcome them into the house, before showing them into the study. Then while I made a drink he would talk to them. I thought this was probably very good for their ongoing pastoral training!

Another change that occurred concerned the way Adrian began to follow me everywhere. If I left the living room to go to the kitchen he would follow; if I left the bedroom to go to the kitchen he would follow; if I went into the garden or the study he would follow. So if I needed to talk to someone in the study he would try to follow. I would often find myself meeting the dogs and Adrian in the doorway coming towards me as I returned. I needed to find a new way of dealing with this difficulty.

I was beginning to realise that it was pointless to tell Adrian to stay where he was, for he would do this for a moment but then come to look for me. I also noticed that his levels of anxiety increased immediately, if I left him alone. He appeared to be trying to work out where I was going and how long I was going to be missing, which heightened his anxiety. So I needed to find some way of helping him to stay where he was, something that would keep him content when I left the room for a few moments to make a cup of tea, or to wash my hair. At this point I knew I was going to have to stop working soon, for being away from Adrian for an hour was far too long for him to cope. However, I did need to find some way of being absent for ten minutes or so, if life at home was to continue in any normal fashion. After all there were times when I wanted to go to the bathroom, if nothing else.

I began to give the whole problem some real attention. Firstly, I needed to think about the whole difficulty from Adrian's perspective. If I left a room, how would he feel? He would be alone, although at this stage he knew he was at home, but he wouldn't know why he was on his own or where I had gone. What would he do then? Obviously he would go and search the bungalow to find me, and this is what I needed to stop him doing. So it all boiled down to how I could keep him content in, say, the living room, without him having to search for me.

My solution could not really include just words, since Adrian was unable to remember these for more than a moment. It occurred to me that although I must find some words, I needed to link these to action for the message must make sense to him. However, that wouldn't be sufficient, for I also needed to find something to keep him occupied while I was away from him and possibly some explanation when I returned.

The first of these difficulties, to find something to explain my absence, was simple to solve. If it looked like he was going to follow me then I would ask Adrian if he wanted a cup of tea or coffee. He would usually just nod and go back to watching the television or whatever he was doing. After some time I didn't need to say anything, instead of asking the question I could go to the door and when he looked up, I would mime drinking

a cup of tea. He would smile and the
allowed me to go out of the room for a f
before he needed to look for a reason fo
At this stage I learnt to return within five
place a tray of tea things in front of hi
teapot. This gave him a visual signal of where I had
gone. Eventually I would return with the teapot and we
would have a cup of tea. While I was away if he began
to wonder where I had gone he would see the tea tray
and think "She's gone to make tea". Reassured he
would go back to whatever he was doing.

This manoeuvre allowed me to go out of any room for
up to twenty minutes, often longer, and I could now do
many of the things I needed to do around the bungalow,
without bumping into Adrian (and the dogs) as I went in
and out of doors. However, for the plan to work, it also
needed Adrian to be relaxed and happy. Watching
television would sometimes achieve this, and I would
record programmes that he enjoyed, to be played when
he was on his own. But I also needed to find more
activities for this policy to work. I came up with a few
ideas, some of which were more successful than others.

Our older son D___ had made a beautiful wooden box
and then filled it with old photographs and objects that
recaptured many incidents from Adrian's life. There was
a picture of him with his brothers when they were
children, another of Adrian in his twenties in RAF
uniform, one of our wedding in 1965, then our sons as
babies, along with snapshots of various places we had
lived in the past. I would leave the 'memory box' on the
coffee table in the living room, usually with the lid open,
so that he could look at it any time he wanted. Over the

onths things were changed or added to the box. I put in a small shield given to him when he won a game of basketball, a little cross to remind him of church, and a shell from the beach which could recall times as a boy at Porthcawl or Barry, although it actually came from the beach on our doorstep.

Another activity that would keep Adrian contentedly occupied for some time, was brushing our two dogs, Toffee and Fudge. If the dogs were in the same room and their brush lay on the coffee table, after a while I would only need to lift the brush, look at Adrian and raise an eyebrow and he would respond happily. I learnt not to leave the hard metal-spiked brush which neither dog really liked, but to put down the soft one which they did enjoy. They thought they were being cuddled rather than brushed, and would stay happily leaning against his knee as he stroked them with the brush.

These activities seemed to stop Adrian entering the cycle of thinking and questioning that would often leave him in a state of panic because he couldn't find an answer as to where I had gone and why he was alone. The biggest worry for me concerned his habit of looking further afield if he couldn't find me, for this would take him out onto the road. The look in his eyes when I found him would be truly awful. He looked like a small child standing in the middle of a world that had gone mad.

CHANGING OUR LIFE

Sometimes my strategies worked, sometimes they did not. I got better at judging what would be successful and to reappearing after half-an-hour with a reason for why I had left. I couldn't depend upon Adrian remembering why I had gone out of the room, so sometimes I would invent another reason to return. The reason didn't need to be spoken. If I appeared wearing an apron he would ask if I was cooking or if I came in with a book he would assume I had been working in the study and had now finished. I also became adept at putting myself down, and taking the blame where necessary, so that he always felt in charge of the situation.

One of the best solutions for reappearing was to come into the room and say, "Oh dear, is that where I left the teapot. No wonder I couldn't find it!"

I would then mime drinking a cup of tea, and he would happily nod, completely having forgotten that I had already asked him and had not yet delivered a cup of tea. Another half an hour of peace would occur, leaving me to continue what I needed to do – cooking, cleaning, or talking to others.

In the early days when I didn't judge things correctly the study door would be opened and his head would appear around the door. He would glare suspiciously at the person with whom I was talking, and at this point I would watch to see what would happen. The more astute of my visitors would greet him with great pleasure as though they had known him for ages, and since I had already briefed them about Adrian, would often start a conversation with him. One such incident that comes to mind occurred when a young woman I was interviewing picked up her notebook and smiled at him.

"Just finishing our bible study," she said.

"I can't understand what St Paul is saying," I added.

Adrian shook his head. "Never liked him – a lot of words!" he said, glad that he understood what we were doing. "I'll leave you to it!"

The latter became his phrase every time he found me in a meeting. "A lot of words," he would say smiling, usually followed by "Do you want a cup of tea?"

Reassured he would then leave for at least another fifteen minutes.

At other times if I got it wrong, I would be talking with someone who was sitting in front of the window and see behind them, that Adrian had left the bungalow and was crossing the road. After another meeting that ended with lunch at which Adrian was present, I went to make some coffee and forgot to say where I was going. On my return I discovered that since no-one had engaged him in conversation he had gone off walking down the road, followed eventually at a distance by one of my visitors.

In the first year after our move Adrian wandered over to the Village Hall and put his head round the door where the embroidery class was being held, to find me. I was rather surprised he knew where I was. For some weeks after this he would join the class, before walking home with me. However, eventually those days were long gone and I needed to ensure that he didn't 'escape' from home because it was becoming too dangerous.

Adrian was never run over but during the summer when the traffic became very busy outside our bungalow I did get very concerned. He never took the dogs on these escapades luckily, and other than heading towards the village hall in the early days, he would usually head to the pub a couple of hundred metres away from home. After I had finished working I would wander over the road to pay for his drink if he hadn't taken his wallet. Luckily the owner of the pub and those who were drinking there would care for him until I appeared. They became very adept at listening to him, and allowing him to air his views even if these didn't make much sense to anyone.

For some years I managed to keep Adrian safe without having to lock the front door. I never had to lock the back door as the rear garden was completely fenced. A gate had been put in around the other side of the bungalow, but Adrian never seemed to find that. I placed a padlock on it eventually, so that I only needed to watch the front door. I knew that if he found the door was actually locked it would cause a problem, so I preferred simply to keep a close watch on this access. In the event when it was necessary to lock the door, if he got annoyed, he had usually forgotten what was wrong by the time he found me to expostulate.

Early on in his dementia journey an area of Adrian's life that changed concerned one of his greatest enjoyments. Before he had retired from work he would start around six o'clock in the morning, and take a coffee break around nine o'clock. During this time he would look at the cryptic crossword in a national broadsheet. Most days he could complete this in around nine minutes. Sometimes he would bring the paper home at the end of the day, especially if he'd found it difficult, and our sons learnt how to do these specialised crossword puzzles as they discussed them with him. Over the years they would ring him, or if he were on holiday, they would try to complete the crossword and there would be a debate on the clues he had been unable to complete.

Slowly it began to take Adrian much longer, and the boys noted that he would bring the newspaper back home with the crossword hardly touched. If they tried to work out the clues, he would show a lack of interest, which was unheard of prior to his illness. After a while he would attempt the simpler crossword on the same page, and ignore the cryptic crossword. In the years to come even the easier crossword was rejected as well as the whole notion of reading a newspaper. However for the moment life was fairly happy and we were content to live in the moment.

For the first years after we retired we enjoyed coming together in the afternoon, whatever we'd been doing during the day. One of the silly decisions we made before Adrian retired, was to stop every afternoon for a cup of tea with a ginger 'bicky' dip. Sometimes instead of stopping for a drink at home we'd drive out along the coast to one or other of the cafes in the area either in the hills or by the sea. In Pembrokeshire we continued this habit. We had always done this on my day off or when we were on holiday in the past, and both of us enjoyed just sitting and looking at the beauty of the world around, watching crashing waves on the headland or above the beach, or observing the birds wheeling across us in the sky as we relaxed. In winter we would do the opposite, and light the coal fire to shut ourselves away from the cold winter winds.

COOKING

Another area of our life that had to change concerned cooking our meals. Adrian had done the cooking for the family for most of our married life (that is for at least 45 years) since the time I had spent months in hospital after injuring my back when we lived in Cyprus. Standing for any length of time always brought on back pain, so initially Adrian had taken over shopping, cooking, and ironing for a lot of this time. In the early days he would often cook two separate meals since we each liked different foods at that time. He really didn't like meat (other strangely, than sausages or faggots), although over the years he began to try other food. The day he discovered pizzas when we were on holiday in Turkey for our twenty-fifth wedding anniversary was a real eye-opener. I had never been able to persuade him that they were only made of things he liked, but on holiday and faced only with 'foreign food' as he saw it, he finally succumbed. Pizza became a staple of his diet in the years afterwards. Then finally he began to try meat and would happily eat chicken or beef in the end. This led him to produce his signature dish of a roast dinner most Sundays, with Yorkshire puddings that hit the roof of the oven and roast potatoes with a crispy exterior and soft melting interior.

As Adrian's memory became worse though, I started to work alongside him in the kitchen. At the beginning I simply assisted, preparing the vegetables and seeing that the saucepans didn't boil over, or that food was taken out of the oven when it was cooked. It helped that we were given a steamer around this time. At worst the vegetables would be over cooked, but the steamer refrained from boiling over if the right amount of water was put in initially. I didn't take over all the work in the kitchen for a few years, since Adrian enjoyed cooking and could be trusted to produce a good meal if I just kept a 'weather eye' on him. I had always cooked when we had friends round for a meal, in order to include something like a curry or lasagne. When I did step in to take over more of the cooking, Adrian seemed to accept my sudden interest as normal, perhaps because we were now doing so much together and he was enjoying my companionship.

GARDENING

Another change in our lives however brought with it a role reversal. I had always loved gardening although my work-life balance often meant it had to be left to look after itself. It could be particularly difficult in the spring and autumn when more work needed to be done, and I would find myself watching sadly as the garden got out of hand, knowing I was too busy to get outside. This also occurred if my back was particularly painful, and I might be unable to do the physical work for some weeks.

Over the years Adrian had always done the mowing, but now I needed him to dig the vegetable patch and help clean the greenhouse. I had plenty of seedlings ready to be planted out, but nowhere to put them. The question for me became one of how to ask Adrian to help, without actually asking him! I decided to use my back and his kindness as the catalyst.

One sunny spring day I announced to Adrian. "I'm going to dig the veggie patch this morning!"

He said nothing, but looked a little sceptical as I was still holding my back when I stood up. However, I gathered up my gardening tools from the shed and he and the dogs predictably followed me outside. The patch had been dug the previous autumn, but was now full of weeds that needed to be removed before I could put the bean and pea seedlings into the ground. I put my foot onto the spade and pushed it deep into the soil. So far so good it felt quite friable and soft! However, when I went to lift the spade I was aware that my back gave a twinge and I groaned slightly, not sure if I was going to be able to dig one row, let alone the entire plot.

Adrian had been playing with the dogs on the patio, but heard the sound I made, and turned to look at me. Before I knew it he had taken the spade from me and was enthusiastically attacking the ground with his best shoes on, and some good trousers! Now he was an erratic if eager helper, with absolutely no knowledge of flowers or vegetables, and even less concerning what was a weed. His idea of digging was just to start anywhere, there was absolutely no system. It meant that weeds would often be left behind covered by fresh soil, ready to pop up again after a shower of rain. I would always need to go over it again later if I was to grow vegetables in the ground. However, since he would have done the hard work it was usually a simple job for me to finish the plot. I was very grateful for his help this particular morning though, even if I had to re-dig the ground at some point in the future.

The next day Adrian also took on the mammoth task of cleaning the greenhouse. I had not really done this properly in the autumn and both inside and outside of the greenhouse needed attention, before I could transfer some seedlings that I had grown on the window sill in the bungalow. I started to empty out all the old pots, and he joined me to do the heavy lifting. Then I started to fill a bucket with some water and Jay's fluid. When he saw me take a large sponge out of the shed he happily took it from me, and started to work while I went to attach the hosepipe to the tap.

After an hour he had finished the inside and was attacking the outside of the greenhouse. Here there was a lot of moss and I climbed the ladder to remove it from the top panes with an old knife, leaving him to bend and deal with the bottom glass. As we finished cleaning each section we used the hose-pipe to remove the rubbish on the glass. The first time the hose-pipe was applied however, Adrian got drowned as the water bounced back onto him. The morning ended up with a hilarious water fight between us as we rinsed the glass, accidentally spraying one other. By the time we had finished we were giggling and very wet, but had enjoyed our time working together.

GETTING OUT

A few weeks after this we decided to take a day off and go for a walk in nearby woods with the dogs. Since we'd retired we made sure that we took time out of the ordinary week (not just our afternoon cup of tea), as though we were having a day off. It was all too easy we discovered, just to continue day after day with the routine of living, and our normal activities at church. Weekends and Bank Holidays came and went and we hardly noticed them, indeed sometimes we were caught out, wondering why the library or certain shops were closed, only to discover it was a Bank Holiday weekend. Also, despite living in such a beautiful part of the world, we seemed to have stopped going out to explore the places around us. The only time we saw the sea was accidentally on the way to the shops or coming back from church, which seemed crazy when we lived in such a beautiful part of the world.

So one glorious spring day we decided to take the dogs out and spend an hour or two walking in the woods before going out for lunch. Toffee and Fudge escaped from the car almost before the boot was opened and disappeared down the path to snuffle under the trees and chase after interesting smells. Whenever we explored these woods they always disappeared which made Adrian somewhat concerned, but then one dog would pop up, crossing the path way ahead of us, followed shortly afterwards by the second dog, and he would relax realising that they hadn't become lost.

On returning to the car and putting two muddy dogs into the boot we drove down to Lawrenny Quay where there is an award-winning café which we had been to many times before. I was hoping to have one of their wonderful crab salad meals which I always enjoyed. As we approached the tiny community at the end of the narrow lane, with its boat-yard and sailing club, the tide in the estuary was in and sailing boats were lazily criss-crossing in front of the cafe. As I parked the car Adrian looked around at the idyllic scene, his face alive with curiosity.

"Where are we?" he asked, with interest. "We've never been here before!"

I looked at him to see if he was joking, for he had an incurable sense of humour, but he was absolutely serous. He simply didn't remember that we had visited the café many times before. Sometimes we sat inside the small building (which looked a little like a temporary classroom) if the wind was coming off the water and it was chilly, and at other times we sat outside at one of the tables under an umbrella when the sun was shining. The café was open all the year round. Sometimes out of season the cafe was quiet, and at other times, especially in the summer, the place could be extremely busy. Yet now Adrian could not remember our previous visits!

I bit my tongue to stop myself exclaiming in astonishment at his response. If I made any such comment it would only confuse him, and lead to a period of silence or even depression as he thought about what had happened. He would begin to question why he could not remember going to the Quay or possibly whether he believed me. Thinking on my feet I decided it was best to try and distract him (just like a toddler I remember thinking again), so I pointed out how atmospheric a boat with a red sail looked, as it came down the estuary straight towards us.

From this time on I seriously began to think about getting Adrian the help that he so obviously needed. However it was to be some time before I solved the problem of how to get him to go and see a Doctor and secondly how his difficulties were to be explained, for he would not mention them himself.

USING THE BUS

But, things were not all gloom and doom at this time and one new event in our lives that did work well began over the next few months. Adrian began to travel on his own using the local buses and his free bus pass. He would go to Haverfordwest which was over an hour's journey away by bus, and he enjoyed discovering where else the local buses could take him. I learnt not to worry too much about whether he would return, but made sure that he had a note of his name, address, and telephone number, in his wallet. Hopefully if a difficulty occurred someone would find the note and return him home. On only one journey did he accidentally take a wrong bus, and when he returned home he was jubilant at sorting out the problem for himself. He had gone into Tenby, and on trying to return home he had accidentally travelled to Saundersfoot, rather than towards Pembroke. The buses all pulled into the same bus-stop and it was sometimes difficult to actually see the number or destination of the bus, and he had forgotten to check. However, arriving in Saundersfoot he managed to find the right bus to go back to Tenby and from there to our home. He arrived back very late, but totally triumphant. It did a lot for his confidence at this time.

DIY WORK

During this period of our life though, some things did have to be re-adjusted. Adrian had never been a DIY kind of man, but he would mow the grass, mend fences if they fell down, and replace plugs. Slowly, however, he began simply to ignore what needed doing, and later to struggle when they needed repairing. Mark, our friend from Worcestershire, reminded me that he also kept on saying "We need to put oil in the mower". This had always puzzled me, because the diesel mower we had at the time had nowhere to put oil. He was in fact remembering the old two-stroke machine we had used in the past, rather than the diesel mower in present use.

One particularly stormy night the fence by the back door blew down. Where we lived the south-west wind came straight off the sea and could be very fierce. Adrian put his head outside the back door, looked with interest at the damage in the morning, and then turned round and went back inside to watch television. He seemed totally unconcerned and to have no concept of how important it was to replace the fence, before our two dogs escaped. It wasn't that he didn't care, but he didn't seem to know that he should care. Yet until the fence was repaired I would need to put the two dogs onto their leads as they left the kitchen, and then take them from the side door to the back garden every time they wanted to go out. I would also need to make sure that they didn't escape through the broken fence. It was going to very difficult to keep the dogs safe until it was repaired since Adrian was likely to just open the door and let them out, as had been our custom. I was also likely to get very wet when the storms swept in from the west.

Later in the day Adrian did go back outside and propped a panel against the damaged fence. Unfortunately the Pembrokeshire wind would demolish that in one gust during the night. I thanked him for his thought, then went outside and tied the panel in place, hoping it would keep the fence safe for a few more hours. I consoled him with the thought that the fence had needed repairing for some time, and that probably our friend could look at the whole area and ensure it was made safe. We might also take the opportunity to re-order the whole section I suggested. The area just outside the side door would make a lovely seating area with pots full of flowering plants, once the new fence was finished. This thought cheered us both up.

I was able to sort the fence by the back door during the summer when Mark and Jane came to stay and we created an enclosure. There was no gate, and the dogs were now trapped in the back garden even if the kitchen door was left open at any time. Of course it did mean that there was no access from the road to the garage, but when had the car ever been parked in the garage? In due course I was able to fill the area with pots and it made a nice patio area with a table and chairs. We cut out a hole in the fence for the oil man to put his pipe through to fill up the tank behind the garage. The back garden could still be accessed by a gate on the other side, but I put a lock on this. I knew that the front door could in due course be 'controlled' by locking it and removing the key, but that time had not quite arrived yet.

On thinking about the episode of the fence panel I realised what had affected me most was the fact that Adrian didn't seem to realise how important it was to have a safe back garden. This aspect of dementia always caught me out. One of the things that had always impressed be about Adrian, from the moment of meeting him, had been his ability to observe and make connections. He would always notice if someone had their hair cut, if things were moved around in the house, or if I was wearing a new item of clothing. Nothing would escape him, I never had to point out any change, he was always on the ball! Now, his powers of observation had diminished, and together with an inability to remember the near past, it was making his life and mine difficult.

In the New Year during another storm the roof of the shed flew off. The whole shed had been on its last legs when we took over the bungalow and it was surprising that it had lasted so long. I asked a neighbour to help put some new roofing felt onto the shed. He knew Adrian was finding things difficult, but was very thoughtful in getting him to assist by holding the large strips of felt down. The wind was very strong that day, and it took two of them to make it all safe. Adrian hammered the nails back where the neighbour indicated. His work looked a little rough and ready, but was perfectly serviceable when it was finished. However, he was very quiet all evening, obviously aware that he had sometimes done this kind of work on his own before and there had never been a need to ask someone else to organise the help. I took the opportunity to remind him that D___ had assisted him to put a shed roof back on when we lived in Suffolk, which had also been near the sea, some years earlier. It was always a two person job, because of the strength of the wind in both places. This partially reassured him, and he seemed to forget the incident fairly quickly.

ODD THINGS START TO HAPPEN

During this year various 'accidents' began to occur. The first concerned the front door. A couple of times the door was left open and our two chocolate Labrador dogs escaped to cross over the road to the farm on the opposite side. The road could be extremely busy in summer, and living at the end of the village cars very often ignored the 30 mph speed limit. Toffee and Fudge always headed for the wonderful animal smells coming from the farm, and could usually be rounded up fairly easily, but we were lucky that they were not knocked down since they shot out of the front garden like bullets out of a gun in their desire to escape. One weekend they were seen hot-footing it down the road trailed by two elderly ladies in a motor-home, who were scared the two dogs would get run over. Luckily I saw them and retrieved both dogs.

I also noticed that on a few occasions the oven didn't get turned on. Sometimes we would sit down to a very late meal. This didn't concern me much, for we always ate eventually. If the oven was off and our meal late I would make light of the difficulty on each occasion.

"Sorry, AD! I must have turned off the oven," I would exclaim, taking the blame, so that he would smile at my mistake.

"Never mind, we can eat later!" he would say.

The oven was also sometimes left on, but to be fair I was all too aware that I too sometimes left the cooker on, after serving dinner. But it was always easier if it was 'my fault' so Adrian didn't go into that cycle of worrying why he had forgotten to turn the oven off. I was also concerned that the top of the electric cooker was occasionally left on, and that Adrian might accidentally put something onto the electric hob. If so the house would have been on fire. Even with a heat and a smoke detector, and insurance, this was definitely something to be avoided.

All of these changes to our life occurred before Adrian had been diagnosed with dementia, and most well before he went to the Doctor for the first time to try and find out what was wrong. It was three years from the first signs of memory loss before I managed to get Adrian to go and see a Doctor.

7. VISITING THE DOCTOR FOR THE FIRST TIME

All of these different incidents which happened over a period of three years slowly began to stiffen my resolve to speak to Adrian about his memory loss, and encourage him to get medical help. However, it seemed to me that I had four problems, firstly, to get him to speak to me about the difficulties he was having; secondly, to persuade him to agree to go to the Doctor; thirdly, physically to get him to the Surgery; and fourthly work out how to attend the appointment with him. All of these felt like herculean tasks, even though Adrian was such a mild and gentle man. If he had been aggressive and violent, I am sure it would have been even more difficult. The more I looked at the problem the less I could see how I was going to achieve success.

Throughout our married life I had never gone to the Doctor with Adrian. For many years the RAF Medical Centre dealt with all his health matters, and after he left the Royal Air Force, although he was registered with a local practice that was in Gloucester where he worked, not where we had our home. Unless he was called in for a diabetic check, Adrian would avoid going anywhere near a Surgery. I think this stemmed from a problem he had suffered while he was in the RAF. When we lived in Norfolk he attended the Medical Centre every three months and they would check his blood pressure, his sugar levels, and his weight. After this the Doctor would see him, and proceed to read him the riot act about his weight. This meant that the next time he visited the Doctor his blood pressure would go up before he even entered the Surgery, since he was anticipating another lecture. Adrian always felt hard-done-by because the Doctor himself was excessively overweight and he felt it was the 'pot calling the kettle black'! From this time on he became very wary of Doctors.

I had no idea of how to initiate the subject with him so that he didn't immediately shut the whole conversation down. The last difficulty of how to persuade Adrian to let me see the Doctor with him was also going to be paramount. Unless I actually saw the Doctor as well, no mention would be made of his memory problems. I was quite sure he would avoid bringing up the subject. Somehow I must find a way of circumventing the world of medical confidentiality and make sure that the Doctor would deal with both of us at the same time.

I spent a year worrying about these questions, and I was to spend a few more months thinking it through before I put my plan into action. Finally a solution came to me. I would write to the Doctor the week before making an appointment at the Surgery explaining that Adrian was having memory problems, and then basically I would barge in to his appointment with him. It felt like a reasonably good idea. Unfortunately the appointment with the Doctor was to be a complete disaster and put back our joint dementia journey by two more long years.

The Surgery was struggling to find sufficient Doctors at the time I made the appointment in July, and a Locum Doctor was the only person available. I duly wrote to the Head of the Practice asking them to pass on the letter to the Doctor concerned. When Adrian's name was called we entered the small room together. I did glance at Adrian but he didn't seem confused, and he had not queried attending the Surgery or baulked at his name being called. So far, so good, I thought.

As the Doctor welcomed us, I managed to say quickly. "My husband's having problems with his memory!"

She immediately greeted Adrian, and I was unable to remind her of the letter, as she completely ignored me after this. Indeed it seemed from the way the interview continued that she had no knowledge of my letter. It was probably still stuck in someone's in-tray, and had certainly never been passed onto the Locum Doctor.

Less than five minutes later we were out of the Surgery and Adrian had been informed "There seems to be nothing wrong with your memory". He was pleased, but I suspect he was puzzled why we had gone to the Doctors and what had just been said.

The Doctor didn't ask Adrian whether he thought he had any problems, but informed him that she had just received a set of fresh questions to ask anyone who thought they had memory difficulties. She brought out a card with ten simple questions.

I felt slightly hopeful at this point. He would be unable to answer the questions. He couldn't remember what he had done the previous day, or what he'd eaten for breakfast! My only concern was how he would react to being asked the questions, since questions often caused confusion in his brain. I hoped he wouldn't be too upset.

So the Doctor read the questions, and to my complete amazement he didn't cause any fuss, but promptly answered them all correctly.

"Who is the monarch?" she asked.

Well as an ex-member of the RAF until he was fifty-five years old, and sworn to obey the Queen, he had no problem with this answer. He simply dipped into his past memory of swearing loyalty to the monarch, and the pictures of the Queen that had presided over every Mess he had ever been in, and answered correctly.

A question about the year he had been born was answered just as easily, along with other questions about the past. However, if he had been asked where he lived at present, or what he'd done the previous night, the outcome would have been very different. Adrian could have given an hour's lecture on his life as a boy growing up in the Welsh valleys; or about his first school; or his relationship with his three brothers at that time. But the questions he was asked by the Doctor didn't address someone with a failing 'near-present' memory. The past was perfectly clear to him it was the 'near-present' that caused him problems.

As we left the Doctor's Surgery a few minutes later I was unsure whom I was most angry with – the particular authority for the stupidity of the questions; the Doctor for not appreciating how difficult it had been to get Adrian to turn up at the Surgery (he had refused to attend earlier in the day); or Adrian for getting ten out of ten answers correct! It was to take another two full years before Adrian was diagnosed with dementia, by which time things were extremely difficult at home, and neither of us had any help during the early stages of his disease.

8. DAILY LIFE AND SOLVING NEW PROBLEMS

Life for both of us went on much as normal from the summer of 2012, except that I felt somewhat depressed and unsure what on earth I should do now that the issue of Adrian's memory loss had not been addressed. I was still busy, leading a university theology group and nurturing possible new clergy. Although I had retired from full time work, I was a member of the church choir, and periodically had meetings to attend. Then the Vicar was taken ill just before Christmas, and so for almost eighteen months, although retired, I took over three parishes. Another four month stint would occur after this.

LEARNING TO STOP ASKING QUESTIONS

Somehow I needed to reconcile the difficulty of looking after Adrian with doing other work. I needed to help keep him stress-free, and to make his life as interesting as possible. I therefore began to address difficulties as they occurred.

I had noticed that asking him questions could upset him, hence my surprise at the way he had coped at the Surgery. Questions often require us to refer to our past. A query about whether we want to go food shopping will probably force us to think about what food there is in the house, when we last shopped, and what groceries are needed now. For someone unable to think about the near past such a question is terrifying.

Obviously we use questions for many more things. Asking "Are you ok?" will require referencing the immediate past, so will "Did you hang out the washing?" or "Have the dogs been out today?" For a person able to remember things that happened forty or fifty years ago, but not the previous twenty-four hours, none of these questions were easy to answer. The result is often depression, anger, or a desire to ignore what is being asked.

I realised that I had a habit of asking Adrian a question when I returned home after being away for the day. For example, if had been completely normal to walk into the house put my head round the door and ask Adrian "What have you been up to today?" We would then share news over a cup of tea and a ginger biscuit. But asking such a question now would elicit a worried frown and sometimes a blank look, as he sought to remember if there was anything special that had happened.

Another question that would bring the anxious look into his eyes might be if I asked him if anyone had rung while I was out. He would be unable to remember, and he didn't always write down the name of anyone ringing. Such a question would often cause Adrian to be depressed and quiet for the rest of the day, and what had been best avoided at first, now became a definite 'no-no'. I needed to discover a way of finding out information without asking him questions.

I realised that I had learnt something in my past that might help. Adrian and I had looked after my mother many years earlier. She lived with us after having had a massive stroke, which badly affected her body, but not her speech or understanding. Indeed once she was in her wheel-chair she would answer the phone for me while I was out, taking messages from parishioners.

When I returned I would ask a similar question to the one I asked Adrian:

"What have you been up to, today?"

It was a silly question really since she had been sitting in a chair all day, and I quickly realised that it was useless to expect my mother to bring something new to our conversation. She had been inactive all day, whereas I often had lots of interesting things to tell her from the events of my day. The conversation could became very one-sided, with me talking and her listening, but it had the effect of making me be creative in what subjects I brought back. I began to tell her interesting anecdotes and stories that I had accumulated from other people during the day.

So instead of asking a question that Adrian couldn't answer, now I used the same technique. I would return home and mention things that had happened to me, or sometimes things I had heard on the radio, or that others had told me, especially if they would appeal to him. I thought about what subjects had always been important to him, trying to key into his interests, or find things that would appeal to his sense of humour. I concerned myself with 'feelings' not 'facts', asking myself what would interest him.

Meeting parishioners most days I picked up lots of interesting stories. I met those with dogs and cats who often had funny things to tell me about their animals; I learnt strange historical facts about the villages we lived in; I told him about events happening in the primary school; and I kept him up to date with odd things that happened in the surrounding villages. All of these helped to preserve his observational powers, and keep his brain active. For a long while he would still ask about something that had happened, perhaps about a dog or other animal.

FINDING INTERESTING SUBJECTS FOR CONVERSATION

The need to bring back interesting things to talk about made me think about what subjects might interest Adrian. The following came out of this reflection. At this stage they were not in any particular order. I couldn't, for instance, identify one particular theme that might underpin them all. Eventually, I was to find that one single theme, but not for a couple of years. It was to be 'The Computer and work':

- Dogs
- Crossword puzzles
- Children
- The RAF
- Computer and work
- Rugby
- Cyprus
- The family
- The sea and the beach

Over the years this list was to change slightly, some subjects disappearing and others entering, but it was largely to remain the same for a number of years. As his dementia grew much worse subjects began to 'drop off the list' until finally only the main one was left.

Working out these major interests was extremely helpful. I discovered that if I could tap into his memories and concerns without actually asking him a question, then we could have a valuable conversation. Over the years many interesting things had happened to Adrian or to both of us, and anything that touched on these subjects would encourage him to talk about the experience. For example, even when his dementia was very severe, a mere three months before going into the Nursing Home, he participated in a conversation with some students.

While holding a class with a visiting teacher to learn some basic New Testament Greek in our home, Adrian who had been sitting quietly in the room suddenly began to expound quite eloquently on the Greek language, and what he had learnt while living in Cyprus. He had understood that we were learning Greek, although not realised it was New Testament Greek. Nevertheless he made a valuable contribution to the class from his armchair in our dining room where the class was being held. The subject had touched a chord in him, and he was able to participate in the conversation. What was even more impressive was the way the tutor dealt with him as though he were her brightest student giving an impressive display of his talent.

Mention of children, dogs, or rugby always went down well, so I would save up any interesting incidents that occurred during my working day, or alternatively mention things I had heard on the news to tell him. I would also gather funny or amusing stories, embroidering slightly on what I had heard. In the first year after he had retired, while I was still working, it was simple to cheer him up because although he had been alone for much of the day he was more active, still taking the dogs out and going to the shops.

In later years it was even more important to help Adrian have subjects that he could engage with, and that helped to keep him positive and confident. Often he would forget the 'news' that I had brought him half an hour later, and sometimes I would be able to tell the same story again, giving him an equal amount of pleasure as before.

One afternoon I came in having seen a few sheep that had escaped from a field on the way back from Haverfordwest, and retold him another story about sheep. We had called it the 'incident of the sheep', and it was something that happened to me while we'd been living in Cumbria! He didn't remember the incident, but was happy for me to retell it one again.

Our home then had been on a hill surrounded by fields containing hundreds of sheep, with a cattle grid at the entrance to the Vicarage. On leaving that morning I discovered about a dozen sheep in the lane outside. They had apparently escaped from one of the fields and were running down the road. Almost opposite our house was a gate that had fallen over. There were never any sheep in this particular field, so I knew they hadn't come from there, but it occurred to me that it might be a good place to herd them. I parked my car across the middle of the road which stopped them continuing down the steep hill and then tried to get them to enter the field. However they had to cross the gate lying on the ground, and they didn't like the look of the fallen gate. I flapped my hands wildly at them. At first it didn't look as though they'd move, but finally after a few moments of hysterical 'shepherding' I managed to get all the sheep into the field. Now came the question of how to contain them! I bent to pick up the gate only to discover it might look light but it was in fact extremely heavy. I was only able to lift it to the height of my knees. So there I stood, bent over (with a bad back), struggling with all my might to hold up this enormous gate. It was no good I couldn't put it back into place. I would have to lay it down again. Then I saw that the sheep were coming towards me, trying to get out of the field. A massive final heave took the gate to the level of my chest. But how was I to keep the gate upright? If I left the gate it would simply fall over and the sheep would escape. The solution was to wave my arm at a total stranger in a car and ask them to hold the gate while I went over the road to home to get some rope to ensure the gate stayed put.

By the time I'd told him of the 'incident with the sheep' Adrian was laughing, as I embroidered the tale of how I was nearly laid out flat by a huge gate. It kept him occupied for a long while. He finally remembered something about the story for he asked if people had sent me cartoons and postcards with sheep on them after that, which in fact they had. I also noticed that if I mentioned sheep after this he would remind me of my piece of shepherding. It was a memory that Adrian kept for a long while. Even when his dementia was fairly advanced he would still occasionally remember the incident.

Another way into a meaningful conversation was to let Adrian initiate or guide the direction of any talk. Sometimes something I started would be continued on a different tack by him, although it was usually connected to the past. I would then try seamlessly to go along with what he had begun. After all he had always been better at remembering the past than I had. His memories of years ago were as sharp and clear as if they had just happened. So talk about high winds and heavy rain during the day, for example, would lead him to remember a time in Cumbria in the past when a car door had blown shut breaking an elderly lady's arm. On another occasion after a very windy day he mentioned a particularly bad crossing we'd had when travelling from Northern Ireland some thirty years previously. He reminded me that I'd left a book by Georgette Heyer that I was reading, in the cabin. I had completely forgotten this, but Adrian's memory for the past was quite clear about the event. Both these conversations were occasioned by me coming in and telling him how bad the wind was that day.

In the first few years of our retirement, however, there were times when I forgot my policy of not asking Adrian questions, and I would initiate the conversation with a question as to his day. This would bring on that slightly quizzical, slightly vacant look that I was beginning to recognise and dread. It was a look that meant he was trying to make sense of what I had asked him, but was struggling to remember what he had done during the day, and wondering why he couldn't remember. That would push him further into a dark mood. Sometimes it would be hours before I could retrieve the situation, and sometimes it would last until the next day. He would just sit quietly, not speaking, but there were no jokes or smiles until he came out of the mood. I worked hard at helping him to keep some kind of equilibrium so this didn't happen too often.

Late one January afternoon though when I noticed that Adrian was putting on his thick coat, I became concerned. "Where are you going?" I asked, forgetting I shouldn't ask him a question, my mind already going through the possible answers - the pub, or walking the dogs?

He turned from putting the dogs back into the kitchen – so no walk for the dogs, I concluded.

"I thought I'd get the bus and go and collect the dry-cleaning," he said, checking he had his bus pass in his wallet. "Have you got the ticket for the cleaners?" he asked.

My heart sunk, there was no way this was going to be easy. "We could do it tomorrow, and I could take you into town?" I responded, trying not to tell him it was Sunday and there were no buses.

There was a slight pause, while he thought about what I had said, before he answered. "Oh! Alright! I can just as easily do it tomorrow."

"Why don't we give the dogs a walk instead?" I asked. "They haven't been out for some time. We could go down to the beach. It's not a bad day for January."

Immediately his attention was side-tracked, and he was content. Boredom had been the problem. It was a beautiful winter's day, and he didn't know what to do with himself. We subsequently spent a happy afternoon throwing a ball for Toffee and Fudge, while attempting in vain to stop the former from eating as much seaweed on the beach as she could, and the latter from jumping the waves and drinking the salt water, which only upset her stomach. We returned tired, but happy. Disaster had been averted!

Over the years the things that interested Adrian didn't change much, as I said, but the original list grew shorter. Finally the subject that he mostly wished to talk about concerned his work for the RAF, and since none of the family really understood that much about 'main-frame computers' it became difficult to participate in his private conversation. We knew he was talking about work, but it usually concerned the programmers, or instructions that needed to be given to them concerning the payroll on the computer.

His interest in children and dogs and his enjoyment in the company of women remained through almost to the end of his life. He would happily sit with our granddaughter looking at a book with her, long after he could make any sense of the book. He would also stir himself to try and communicate with any baby or small child that came near to him.

Throughout these years without realising it I was becoming adept at shielding Adrian from his own mistakes. I would give him tasks that he could achieve that would help feed his sense of self-worth and bolster his self-esteem. When anything became difficult I found easier jobs that he could do, ensuring that he still felt wanted and loved. In retrospect, if I stopped to think, I was able to see how the goals continually changed over the years. However, at the time I often preferred not to notice the changes that were occurring.

NEW PLACES ARE DIFFICULT, OLD PLACES ARE COMFORTABLE

At the beginning of February 2012 we both travelled to Keele to help K___ our younger son move in to a flat on the university campus. I had thought Adrian would be in his element – pick up a box or a piece of furniture, carry it for thirty yards and then up to the second floor; back down to the van, and start all over again. He was quite a strong man, and helping to shift the heavy items would be no problem for him. This was just what we needed, since I had a bad back and heavy lifting wasn't easy for me.

However, I had not accounted for the fact that Adrian was unable to decide what item to pick up, and exactly where he had to go. Even after the first five or six visits to the flat he was unable to find his way there unless he followed one of us. Neither could he find his way back to the van. After half-an-hour I found him hanging around the van we'd hired. He had found his comfort zone, and seemed unconcerned that we needed his help. I finally left him to bring the heavy items from the back of the van to the tail-gate, before passing them to us. We were luckily rescued by Adrian's brother who lived nearby. At the end of the day over a meal, three of us were totally exhausted from the fifty trips up and down the stairs, while Adrian was happy to talk for hours about memories of his childhood in the Welsh valleys with his brother and his sister-in-law.

This night the question "Do you remember?" elicited no difficulty, because he could remember exactly what happened. Indeed he could add many more memories to those mentioned by his brother. The pictures in his mind were as sharp and clear as if they had just happened. He knew every name, and could describe every situation – the times when they had ridden the wild ponies, or shot at each with air guns when they were playing cowboys and Indians, and that special occasion when he had rescued his youngest brother who had got lost in the mountains. The story went that three of the brothers had been playing on the mountain, and had gone over the other side and down into a valley. The two oldest had lost the younger brother somewhere along the way, and returned home to be met by their mother who pointed her hand back up the mountain.

But the instruction was for the oldest boy, Adrian. "Find him, and don't return until you do!"

So aged nine, at the end of a long day and probably very tired, he went back up the mountain and searched until he found his brother. They returned home in due course. He never said if his Dad had taken a belt to him that night, the chances are that he did. The memory of this story was as clear in his mind as the day it had happened. Adrian had an absolutely wonderful evening and slept well that night.

I remembered this incident a couple of years later when we went on holiday to Devon. By then Adrian was totally unsettled, staying in a holiday cottage, and just wanted to go home. At Keele it was less obvious, but the nevertheless the desire for a place he knew rather than somewhere strange was already present.

At the end of May that year Adrian was totally happy for me to leave him at home where he felt comfortable and safe, while I went on retreat with another woman priest to a Convent near Monmouth for four days. It was a wonderful time, made all the more special because I was aware that I would be unable to leave Adrian alone in the future. I made sure that neighbours unobtrusively checked up on him. He used his bus pass to travel during the time I was away and apparently all was well. I think he enjoyed the space to be alone, to sit and watch television, and to slip over the road to the pub each night to meet his friends.

NEW THINGS TO DO TOGETHER

After returning to Pembrokeshire I began to think about jobs we could do together, where his strength and my mental ability would work best. We had bought some new beds for the spare room before we went away. They were composed of metal rods connected to a metal frame, and each bar had to be fixed with an alun key. Adrian was unable to understand the diagram (and because of his spatial difficulties he had never been able to understand them), but after studying it I could just about work out how the whole frame was put together. I wouldn't have been able to do it on my own though, for the room was small and the beds were heavy, but with Adrian's help and using his strength, we were able to manage. While Adrian held the heavier components I was able to put in the bolts. Then finally Adrian could use his superior strength to tighten each bolt after I had finished. We had a lot of laughs as we tried to turn the frames round in the small space without damaging the paint work or breaking the window. Finally though, we achieved the task of putting together two beds for the spare room. At least we could now have guests to stay in the winter without them having to sleep in a tent or the caravan. Adrian felt very pleased with himself that night, for he knew that he had really been needed to complete the job.

Continuing this thinking, about what we might do together, I contacted the WRVS to see if we might be considered for helping deliver 'Meals on Wheels'. After a few weeks we were both interviewed by a lady from the WRVS. She helped us to fill in all the CRB forms, and we took them into the Council offices. Subsequently they came back, and we were accepted to do the work together, as a team.

After a trial run in August where we were guided by another WRVS volunteer we finally took over our own round, delivering meals each week. We collected the hot food from a school, and delivered it to about a dozen people in Pembroke and Pembroke Dock. The list of houses didn't change much so we grew to know our customers. Adrian would carry the boxes of food to the car for they were not only heavy but were very hot. I would check the addresses, keep an account of the money collected, and generally lead the way to the different properties before returning to the school with the empty boxes. We met some really interesting characters and shared with them our stories. It also did us good to meet people who were far worse off than we were.

We both enjoyed talking to our customers, many of whom were very frail, and we always found ourselves warmly welcomed. Conversations about our two chocolate Labrador dogs, or our grandchildren were natural as customers mentioned their own animals or grandchildren. However as the year went on I needed to watch Adrian more and more. He was likely to step out into the road, and take off in the wrong direction. I solved this by pulling up with the near-side passenger door by the pavement, and not giving him the tray of food until I was ready to leave.

We made it safely through the next year and Adrian thoroughly enjoyed engaging with thirty or so different people. It gave him things to talk about as we travelled between the different homes. We delivered meals on Boxing Day and on New Year as well as our usual day each week, and enjoyed talking to all our elderly ladies and gentlemen. However, after a year I was beginning to find it rather stressful looking after Adrian and keeping him safe when we crossed roads, so we agreed to give up the work.

August proved to be eventful. At the church fete in Manorbier Castle Adrian won first prize in the raffle. He was very pleased for it was £200. It did his morale wonders, and helped to boost his self-esteem. We walked back from the castle to home, the furthest we had walked for some time.

A few days later K___ arrived with his girlfriend R___. She also worked at Keele University as a Lecturer, and lived in a flat below his. I cooked a roast dinner with Adrian's help, and he made some 'mean' gravy. Adrian certainly enjoyed meeting someone new, and her arrival together with K___ lifted his spirits at the time. Two days after they left, Adrian's younger brother and his wife arrived to stay for a couple of days. They had been very helpful when we moved K___ into his new flat at Keele, but they could see the changes in Adrian that had occurred in just the few months since then. Nevertheless there was a lot of laughter and much reminiscing of childhood events in the Welsh hills.

Once Adrian stopped driving I was determined that he would not be imprisoned within our house. I found excuses for driving out to enjoy the beauty of the country and seaside, and to go for walks, or generally just to explore new places in and around Pembrokeshire. We tried every lane and road in the area just to find out where they went, and discovered some interesting footpaths, new seaside coves, and different woods. I also encouraged him to take the dogs out each day, until eventually the local policeman felt he was not controlling the dogs as he should. Then I slowly curtailed this by telling him that I had walked them earlier, or else I would take all of them out, or we would throw a ball in the garden for dogs. As the Labradors were getting to be elderly ladies, they were not too worried if they didn't get the amount of exercise they had been accustomed to receiving.

GETTING LOST

Since Adrian could go anywhere he wanted at this time, there was always the possibility that he would lose his way and get lost. However, only twice did he actually disappear, and the third time this occurred was more of an accident. Each occasion though left me worried and concerned, and the first twice occurred when he was out walking the dogs. One afternoon he set off up the hill behind the house onto the Ridgeway, a long low ridge that prehistorically had probably been an ancient beach by the sea. On reaching this he turned right, aiming to walk along the top of the ridge for a while and then turn back down into the village, past the school and back home. After two hours however, there was no sign of Adrian, and he had not returned home. My mind began to visualise all kinds of scenarios, and I began to worry if there had been a problem with the dogs. So I took the car out onto the Ridgeway to see if I could find him. I didn't want to appear to be spying on him, especially if he had just decided to walk a little further, but I suspected that he'd actually taken a wrong turn.

He was nowhere to be found, certainly not where I expected him at least. I went up and down the Ridgeway, but couldn't see the dogs or Adrian. Finally beginning to panic somewhat I spread my net wider, thinking hard about where he could be, not wanting to start asking other pedestrians if they had seen him. Finally on my second sweep I saw him in the distance, on the road ahead. Instead of turning off and down into the village he had continued along the Ridgeway, making his two mile walk into at least four or more miles. Whether this is what he attended I wasn't sure.

The question now was should I simply allow him to continue, or would he make another wrong turn when he reached the main road and end up halfway to Tenby? I noticed that our elderly dogs and Adrian all looked hot and tired, so I made a snap decision and pulled up behind him. He turned to look at me and pulled the dogs over to the side of the road. He didn't make any comment about why I was there and I just let him think I had arranged to pick him up. In fact he looked somewhat relieved that I was offering to drive him and the dogs home and even happier when I suggested that we might both like an ice cream from the shop in the village. No further mention was made of why he had walked so far along the Ridgeway, and he never did it again.

The second time he became lost also involved the dogs. We had some family staying and had all decided as the weather was reasonable that we would walk to a hidden beach nearby. Although it's possible to drive the first half-a-mile, the rest of the journey must be done by foot as it crosses three fields before dropping down a steep pathway to the cove. We agreed therefore to walk the whole way rather than take the cars.

All went well until we reached the steep climb down to the beach. Adrian didn't feel that his knees were up to this challenge and decided to stay on the path above the bay. The two dogs stayed with him, as we didn't intend to remain long on the beach. However, the weather was warmer than expected down in the hidden bay and we spent some time exploring the rocky outcrops. It was a beautiful day and in the end everyone found a comfortable rock and spent some time basking in the sun in this completely secluded place.

I kept a watch on Adrian and noticed he too had found a large rock to sit on. Periodically I would check him and he appeared content to sit with the dogs watching our activities. However, a while later when I looked up there was no sign of him. I guessed he had probably climbed back up to the top path, and was slowly making his way home. Feeling that I needed to check he was alright, it wasn't long before we all started up the steep climb from the beach, resting occasionally before we tackled the last section of the path. It took some time to reach the first meadow and then finally the road.

Once back on the road though there was no sign of Adrian. I concluded he had obviously turned towards home and by now would be back at the bungalow. Ten minutes later we crossed the road to home, and I expected to see him sitting in the porch waiting for us to unlock the door. However, there was no sign of him. Perhaps he had popped into the pub for a drink? It was certainly hot enough to want to quench one's thirst.

When that proved not to be the case, two of us took to our cars to try and work out where he might have gone. We searched the OS maps to see what other paths he could have taken. If he had walked along the coastal path where might he have ended up? At this point we began to ask holiday-makers if they had seen a man with two chocolate Labrador dogs. An hour later saw us using the binoculars from the top car park above Manorbier to scan the cliff paths. We could see no sign of him, so I drove down to the beach below the castle. He was not there, so I returned to the top of the hill again.

Suddenly I spied him. He was jauntily striding around a distant headland, on a part of the coastal trail. Instead of taking the more direct track back to the road he had managed to do an enormous detour, which followed the coast, although he had finally ended up in the right place. He seemed completely unaware that we had been searching for him. Neither did he question why we had managed to get there before him, or why I was in the car, which we hadn't taken with us. In fact the subject was never mentioned again, for there was no point in taking him to task. We had all learnt not to ask Adrian questions about such things, for it simply upset him, and achieved nothing. As it was he had explored a section of the path that none of us had travelled before, and had thoroughly enjoyed himself. Added to which neither he nor the dogs had fallen off the cliff path, they were all perfectly safe.

Sometime later we attempted the same walk to this hidden bay and again Adrian wouldn't walk down the last bit onto the beach, nor would he let us help him down. However, suddenly he allowed two strangers to almost carry him onto the beach. He then spent an hour happily watching the dogs gambol in and out of the surf, before all of us helped to haul him up again.

I nearly lost Adrian on one other occasion, which amused us all afterwards, although it was scary rather than funny. We were in our friend Anne's car and pulled into a local hotel where I wanted to check a booking for a meal that I had made for my university group. I got out of the car, popped into the hotel, and a few minutes later returned. Getting into the car Anne backed out of the car park ready to go into Pembroke. As we turned onto the road, she suddenly felt a draft. I glanced towards the back seat to discover that Adrian was missing. He must have stepped out just after I closed the car door. I had moved away and didn't notice. Anne said she'd turned up the music on the cd thinking he might enjoy it, so she didn't hear the car door being opened. We found Adrian wandering round the hotel gardens, perfectly happy on his own, exploring the beautiful garden. He didn't seem to notice that we had left him, or that as far as we were concerned he was missing.

After this I made sure that the child locks were applied to the back doors of any car in which we travelled. However, that didn't solve the problem of how to keep Adrian in a front seat. For there were no child locks in the front of the car. I could use the central locking in the car when we were inside, but that didn't actually help, because he could still open it from inside if he wished. On a couple of occasions he tried to open the car door when we were driving somewhere, and I had to slow down instantly, and deal with the problem. Luckily he always had his seat belt on, and since he usually had trouble undoing that, he was fairly safe. However, I did get concerned about the car and about other people. If he had opened the car door while we were moving we could have had a bad accident. I never did manage to sort this problem out, because he wouldn't sit in the rear of a car – to be fair it was really the fact that he had trouble getting into the back seat. So it meant that I needed to keep a constant watch on him while the car was moving.

9. Keeping active and engaged with society

During the early years of our joint retirement we settled into our home and into the new area of Pembrokeshire, exploring our surroundings, and beginning to make some good friends in the parish. Our immediate neighbours were most welcoming and before long we were looking out for one another, something I had begun to realise was necessary as we all grew older. They were to prove very helpful in giving me assistance when I needed it over the years, and early on if I was away they would keep an eye on Adrian. In return I would water their gardens, accept parcels if they were away, order goods on-line for them or make appointments for the Doctor on my computer. Each of us used our own abilities and gifts to help one another. As we also made friends with people in the parish church and in the various village groups we joined, so our social life increased.

We had been in Pembrokeshire for a couple of years when we were invited to a friend's Golden Wedding Anniversary at a local Hotel which lifted both our spirits. Adrian's deafness could sometimes cause problems, for he wouldn't wear his hearing aid, and in noisy social situations his hearing was much worse. However, on this particular night we were sitting at small tables in a marquee which helped. Also there were a number of other ex-servicemen present and Adrian was in his element. Somehow they all managed to hear one another, and the tall stories of past exploits grew longer as the evening progressed. Some of these contacts, along with others made through the local branch of the Royal British Legion, were to prove of great use in helping to stop Adrian becoming isolated and 'shut-in' as his memory grew worse.

He also enjoyed attending the Open Day at the old airfield a mile or two away from us, looking at all the stalls, trying out various pieces of equipment, and watching the aircraft fly overhead. He particularly enjoyed trying on a huge helmet on the stall being manned by the police. It was meant to show people what their sight was like when they were drunk, and it skewed everyone's vision so that when they were walking they ended up in the wrong place, and if they put out a hand to touch something they found they were nowhere near the object.

There were stalls run by the RAF as well as displays about the old station that had been on the site during the war. Being around men and women in uniform cheered Adrian up enormously, and he spent over an hour content to walk around exploring the airfield with some of our family and friends.

Another outing that was not quite so successful was an invitation to dinner one night. Adrian didn't know the couple and didn't engage with any of the conversation. He was in an unknown environment and with strange people as far as he was concerned. Their house was also cold and we had become accustomed to having the central heating on for most of the winter at home. However, the evening was rescued by the arrival of the host's children who came down to see the visitors. Adrian enjoyed talking to them and amusing them, and really came alive while they were with us.

But perhaps the most difficult outing was a lunch held by the church choir. This was not caused by the people present whom Adrian knew quite well, but the way we were seated. Unfortunately we were sitting at long tables, and he was at the end of a row. He was only able to speak to the person next to him or the two people opposite. The person next to him, however, turned towards their neighbour on the other side, effectively turning their back on Adrian, and as he found it difficult to hear the people on the opposite side of the table he was effectively isolated. I made a note that he would be better at a smaller table in future, or else he needed a place in the middle of a long table.

Our life together had always involved inviting people into our home, whether this was holding a dinner party to celebrate something or to thank people for all the work they were doing in the parish. Sometimes we would hold a 'coffee morning' with stalls to help raise money for the church. At other times we would be involved in an 'open garden' event, or a tea-party in the garden. In the last year in Cumbria I well remember a beautiful day and a group enjoying the afternoon in our garden. I had shut the dogs in the kitchen, but I had opened the greenhouse so that people could look in and see what was growing. Two minutes later while I was showing people around, I discovered all the cucumbers in the greenhouse had been eaten – by the dogs - which Adrian had let out! Sometimes while I was looking after the bigger picture at such an event, I would take my eye of Adrian and disaster could occur.

However, on the plus side I couldn't manage such events without Adrian's help. He loved being with people and would chat away to visitors. As well as this he would help to cook food or to set up for an event. In Pembrokeshire when we held a huge coffee morning, that attracted almost more people than we could squeeze into the bungalow Adrian helped me move furniture round, made the tea and coffee, and welcomed everyone that came in that morning. Such an event always left him feeling more cheerful, even if we were both exhausted at the end of the day.

FINDING ACTIVITIES TO DO

But Adrian had never been a man for hobbies and pastimes, indeed his sons and I used to struggle to buy him Christmas and Birthday presents because of this. He wasn't interested in golf or other outdoor activities, although as a younger man he had played rugby, and basketball. Occasionally he would try a new hobby but often it wouldn't last for long. It looked at one time as though photography might be something that would interest him. Anne gave him a camera that had belonged to her husband, but he was unable to master the use of it. In retrospect I should have encouraged him to use a phone to take photographs, which I could then have uploaded onto the computer.

The village we lived in did offer many activities for us to join, either together or separately. In the past when we were both working such long hours it had not been possible to take up such opportunities. Now it was a joy to explore what was on offer in the village hall and the church, and join new clubs, and since Adrian had got into the habit of accompanying me to any event he would happily join in a number of different activities.

While living in Cumbria he had helped to make an Easter garden in one of the churches. We would create a small garden around the font with a group of adults and children, trying to recreate the Garden of Gethsemane, with a cave, a hill and three crosses. Now the same activity on Good Friday grew to huge proportions in Pembrokeshire, taking up almost the whole of the rear of the church. There were paths and a large cave, potted plants to act as trees, fields made of shells and pine cones, and glass jars full of spring flowers. We always needed strong people to help create the hill for the crosses, and to place the heavier items in place. The Easter before Adrian entered the Nursing Home he was still helping a group of us to gather large stones and shells from the beach, and collect fir cones from the woods. He put such large stones into the bucket on the beach, that only he could carry it to the car. Later that week on Good Friday he enjoyed encouraging the children to make the paths and to fill the glass jam jars with flowers for the Easter garden. For six weeks after Easter he helped me to water the plants and flowers, and then finally to dismantle the whole edifice and put all the hard-core super-structure into a cellar to be stored for another year.

Adrian also enjoyed engaging with a number of different crafts in this period. None of these required him to think back to the past, since they were often new things that he was trying. So for example he helped make some banners out of sugar paper. Usually it required two people to create each banner, so he was able to work with another person. It required the couple to create symbols or pictures to fit the theme which were then stuck onto a large sheet of paper. An extra piece of sugar paper was attached to the top and bottom, and finally some means of creating a frame to hang the banner. They were only meant as temporary artwork, but would be bright and cheerful for an Easter or Christmas festival. In Pembrokeshire Adrian was involved in making one of these banners for a church service where we walked around the 'stations of the cross', and he thoroughly enjoyed himself.

One year he joined a group making kites out of thin canes and coloured tissue paper with long tails made of paper twists. After attaching a ball of crochet cotton he went to the beach with others to fly them. They certainly didn't fly like the more expensively bought ones, and some didn't fly at all. However, he and the others had enormous fun making the kites, and congratulating those whose kites did fly.

As his dementia grew worse Adrian's role in these events had of necessity to change, but those around him were sympathetic and adapted to him. Sometimes they would ask him to hold the frame while others applied the tissue paper, and other times he would tie the string ready for flying the kite. Also long before there was any huge evidence of his memory loss Adrian was happy to assist any youngsters struggling to make a banner or a kite. Later they were happy to include him in the activity and help him. The end result was the same – everyone had fun and a wonderful day.

Adrian had always been happy to take part in any drama, although by the time of our retirement he could not handle reams of text. When some of the local churches produced a play based on Bunyan's 'Pilgrim's

Progress' the summer was full of rehearsals. Adrian enjoyed attending these. He had always been a good actor, and in the early years of our marriage had taken major parts in different productions put on by local drama groups. Over the years I had produced a number of plays and musicals and Adrian was always up for a part. We both had wonderful memories of Adrian as Giant Despair many years before – for some reason dressed in black plastic bin-bags – and of Adrian as Uncle William with his arm resting on the pub bar for the whole of the first Act of a rather intense play, speaking in a north country accent, except for the word "year" which always came out in a broad Welsh accent.

In our production of 'Pilgrim's Progress' Adrian was cast as the Judge in Vanity Fair. It was he who would condemn the character of Faithful and send him to his death. I placed a large table with an ornate chair behind it for him to sit on, at the back of the stage. His words were then typed in a huge font and placed on the table in front of him. Adrian had never managed to learn his words properly even when he was in his twenties, and over the years I had constantly lived with the uncertainty of what he would say and whether this would confuse other members in the cast. This time it was no different because now of course he couldn't remember any words. However, he knew he needed to condemn the 'prisoner', unfortunately he was sometimes liable to condemn Faithful a little too early, cutting out the words from other actors. At other times he was far too late, and the whole cast ended up looking to him to say his words. I finally solved the problem by appointing the Judge's Clerk as his assistant

106

and gave the latter a long stick, with which to point to the Judge's words. The play went very well, and Adrian gave a wonderful performance as the Judge, although I suspect that the reason for this was the compassion and concern that everyone showed for him and for his limitations. It did his self-esteem a lot of good, and he enjoyed the whole event.

Another event he enjoyed was his participation in what I called 'postcards' – that is, stationery 'pictures' using real people to tell a story. So the events of the original Christmas were told by a group taking different sections, for example, Mary and Joseph travelling to Bethlehem, the shepherds in the field, etc. Adults and children dressed up in appropriate clothing, and then appeared as static figures at the appropriate time the story was being read. He enjoyed playing various characters, and since there were no words to be learnt, it suited him enormously. The secret, I found, was to put him with someone else to keep him on track.

At home Adrian also used some of his dramatic gift to play charades when our grandchildren came to live with us, and one Christmas he joined the grandchildren, myself and our friend Anne to produce 'The Twelve Days of Christmas' while the song was sung. During this time he also enjoyed playing board games at home. Although the rest of us sometimes colluded and changed the rules to help him, we had done this in the past when the children were young. He particularly enjoyed playing Monopoly with others in the family, although he would cheerfully break all the rules sometimes, knowing perfectly well what he was doing. As time went by he would work with one of the grandchildren as a partner, and still enjoy the whole activity. He was unable to cope with Scrabble, or jigsaws, but would play Connect, Dominoes, and even Cluedo with some help. He would particularly enjoy helping to create or watch marble and domino runs, and card towers. As the family had always helped younger children to participate in such games, now everyone helped Adrian to join in if necessary.

We did have some outdoor activities at this time. We both enjoyed walking, although we were not keen on it as a sport, neither of us being fit enough. In the early days after our move we would walk for a few miles, but over time Adrian's knees began to cause pain and towards the end of his time at home he was none too steady on his feet. However before this, provided the path wasn't too rough he would happily explore a beach or walk in the woods. He loved taking the dogs out, and would spend ages throwing a ball for them, laughing at their antics when they shook water or mud all over him or someone else. With the grandchildren he would endeavour to hide from them and take part in their games in the woods. If they were endeavouring to find ten items of a red colour in the forest, he would search as hard as they did to see who could find the best items, leaving me to judge who had won the game. He would also happily cheat if necessary and argue with our grandson that he had won because the orange piece of paper in his hand was of course, red!

One Saturday when I had to take a wedding, our friends Jane and Mark, took Adrian along with D___ and the grandchildren to a beautiful headland overlooking the Green Bridge of Pembrokeshire (these are beautiful arches in the limestone cliffs) near Castlemartin further along the coast. Adrian was therefore travelling in a strange car, and it took them a long time to get him into the front seat of the car. Perhaps he didn't recognise Jan and Mark that day. When they did get him into the car he kept undoing the seat belt. Jane said it was lucky that she was in the back seat, so she was able to do it up again

Once at the headland there was a steep walk down to the beach, so Adrian stayed with Jane on the headland coast path while the others all went down to walk on the beach.

Suddenly Adrian said, "You know this would make a wonderful place to build a hotel."

After this Jane entered his 'story' and the two of them planned the building of an imaginary hotel and golf course for people to use, so they could see the wonderful view. Adrian finally stopped to talk to some children and wanted to buy them an ice cream. She had to explain quietly to the parents about Adrian's dementia and they were lovely with him. As they walked back to the car park I arrived and we ended the afternoon by all having an ice cream. As far as Adrian was concerned it had been a wonderful afternoon.

Slowly, though if Adrian and I went out alone he was content just to 'be' and we would find somewhere to sit and watch the clouds as they created new shapes, or perhaps we would be intrigued by the waves hitting the cliffs below us, or admire the shape of an intricate shell or stone. Often we would take a flask of tea or coffee and something to eat, and sit in the car on the cliff-top looking out to Caldey Island. Using binoculars we would watch the birds wheeling in and around the cliffs, or the fishermen and visitors in their boats. 'Being' became more important in his life than 'doing', and because of this my life also became less busy as I sat alongside him, taking time to enjoy seeing the world around us, and observing the changing of the seasons.

Dementia forces the sufferer and those around them to live in the present I discovered. Certainly the past is sometimes referred to in order to make sense of what is being seen, but living in the present means there are no real worries about the past or the future. There are no "Why can't I remember?" questions. It is enough to live quietly in the moment – to live as they eventually have to, in the present.

If I found some activities that interested Adrian there was at least one that he never enjoyed, and that was Bingo. In a way it was a shame because it was something that he would have been able to play, perhaps with some gentle assistance, for quite a while. But I think the memories of his mother playing Bingo in the local Miner's Club year after year, had put him off this. However, Snap and its modern derivative that uses different coloured pictures of Mr Bunn the Baker etc certainly kept his interest, and he played this with our granddaughter, along with noughts and crosses, and hangman. Eventually when he began to find it difficult he would play these games alongside one of the grandchildren, against the other child. The three of them would hoot with laughter, and there would be great complaints of "You cheated!" on all sides.

More serious games like golf, tennis and badminton, didn't interest Adrian, although I think he would have been able to play them if he had shown any interest. It would have helped to keep his muscle tone and general fitness levels higher, but it was never possible to persuade him to do something that he was against. He could be a gentle but stubborn man!

Strangely Adrian did enjoy singing, even when he couldn't remember the words. I say this because unfortunately he was tone deaf and couldn't sing in tune. For a Welshman he had an appalling voice! However, as the dementia caught hold he lost his self-consciousness, and was more than happy to sing. Sometimes I could even recognise the tune! In fact towards the end of his time at home in the bungalow he managed to do a lot of singing. The songs of Elvis Presley and Buddy Holly, and other singers of that era were his favourites, and he would sing 'Blue suede shoes', 'Peggy Sue' or, 'That'll be the day' until he ran out of words. But his repertoire also included dozens of hymns. If someone started 'All things bright and beautiful', or 'O little town of Bethlehem' he would happily join in and continue, even if he had to use 'la-la-la' instead of the words. If suitable music were played he would also get up and jive with any woman able to dance to the appropriate music from the fifties. He was to continue doing this long after he had gone into the Nursing Home.

Having said that Adrian didn't really have any hobbies, one of the things that had always interested him had been cooking, and he managed to keep that going for a very long time. He was a good 'basic cook'. He enjoyed cooking ordinary rather old-fashioned British meals – roast dinners with Yorkshire pudding etc. Eventually I had to take over, but even after this he would help me. He would prepare the vegetables, put cake mixture into small cases and then added the decoration afterwards. He would measure out the mixture and still want to flip the pancakes while arguing that syrup was better than lemon and sugar as a topping. This had always been a contentious disagreement in our home.

In the garden and around the house Adrian was invaluable, cutting the grass, preparing and clearing the greenhouse, lifting the heavy pots into place, and collecting the debris from our two cordyline trees. He would gather up the rubbish and help me take it to the local recycling centre, and he would clean the car – although he didn't like this particular job, preferring to get it done at a nearby garage. Adrian would vacuum the carpet, although he never saw the need to dust the furniture, and he would also help me change the bedding. He would wash or dry up dishes, and when needed clean the windows. Sometimes I had to go behind him and finish the job, but more often than not most of this he accomplished on his own up to the last year before he went into the Nursing Home.

THE DIFFICULTY OF STAYING SOMEWHERE STRANGE

During the first few years of our joint retirement we didn't take many holidays, feeling we were on holiday all the time. However, I began to realise that we should go away when we could, and while we were still fairly healthy. We stayed with K___ in Staffordshire and explored the area around there. Adrian was beginning to find it strange to be away from home, but we managed quite well on that occasion. However, a year later things were very different. We had not had a proper holiday that year, and I was beginning to be unsure if he could cope with being away from home. Neither was I sure if I could cope with him on my own, so I invited our friend Anne to join us. We rented a beautiful cottage in Devon, with bedrooms underneath and a lovely open living room and kitchen above. On the first night though the whole holiday almost came to a halt, for Adrian couldn't understand why we weren't going home.

He kept saying "I want to go home!"

That night I struggled to persuade Adrian to go to bed in a strange bed, and began to wonder if I would have to drive home that night. However, I did finally manage to get him into bed in the end. The next morning, though, there was a worried look ingrained on his face, and he was obviously struggling to understand why we had left home. He seemed to have lost the concept of what a holiday was, and why one went on a holiday.

However, once we were out in the daytime he did seem to enjoy exploring the local beaches and countryside, and wandering through the nearby small towns. A couple of times during the week he did ask if we could go home, but he was mostly content. It helped to have Anne with us – another face that he recognised – and he would happily take her hand to cross the road, or wait with her if I went into a shop. I realised, however, that this would be our last holiday together. I also had to accept that he was happier to be at home where he was more likely to be able to find his way around. At home he was able to relax, and the world was less worrying to him.

10. LEARNING HOW TO COMMUNICATE

As time went by, even though Adrian didn't have a diagnosis of dementia, it was obvious to many of us close to him that he needed help. One of the odd outcomes was the way I was learning to assess our friends and acquaintances on how they engaged with Adrian. I wanted to protect him and keep him happy, and to this end it was important to me to make sure I was comfortable with those whom he met.

Some of those we came into contact with in a normal week chose to ignore him treating him as though he weren't present. They would only talk to me. Some of the most surprising people - the educated, and those whose jobs contained a pastoral aspect - seemed unable to communicate with him. It was almost as if he had something that was catching, so they wouldn't appear to notice him, or alternatively they would greet him with an over-hearty "How are you doing old chap," kind of welcome, before immediately turning to speak to someone else. During the last two years of Adrian's life at home some of these people never spoke to him again, even though they had known him for a number of years. I could see how uncomfortable they were in dealing with Adrian. They seemed unable to put themselves in his position.

Because of this I began to write down some of the things that helped make communication with Adrian easier for me, and I shared these with others who were happy to visit him. These were aids to help us all to engage in conversation with him, and they worked for us. They might work for others:

CONVERSATION STARTERS

- Try using a general conversation starter – from subjects that interest them.
- This 'opener' can be used each time.
- Smile at the person, using your eyes as well.
- Eye contact is important – it might take time to achieve.
- Try taking their hand and stroking it – normal inhibitions of doing such a thing often don't apply.
- Don't expect them to know who you are – even if you have known them for years, they may well still treat you as a stranger.
- Don't ask questions – turn questions into statements.
- Offer choices.
- Allow the dementia sufferer to steer the conversation, and go with them even if what they say makes little sense. Use what they say to continue the conversation.
- Don't disagree with them.
- Concern yourself with feelings and emotions rather than facts.
- If the sufferer doesn't want to speak, try speaking to someone else, they may try to join in the conversation.

Friends who tried out these suggestions found they worked, and helped to keep Adrian engaged with the world and at peace, at least as much as was possible.

GROUPS HAPPY TO ENGAGE WITH ADRIAN

Thinking about ways of communicating with Adrian made me look those who were happy to engage with Adrian, often in the same way that they always had. The first of these had been a small group of ladies who went swimming in a small private pool built by a local farmer, in Cumbria. Initially I swam with them, before suggesting that Adrian might like to join the group. He was unsure at first, but finally was persuaded to go swimming. It was something he was to enjoy. His growing dementia didn't affect his ability to swim, and everyone was most welcoming.

The second group were the friends that he met each week at the pub in Cumbria, and later those he met in the local pub a few hundred metres away from our bungalow in Pembrokeshire and who welcomed Adrian right up to the time when he went into the Nursing Home. They treated him exactly as they always had; they would listen to him; include him in their discussions; and generally welcome him into their midst with great compassion. If he had no money because he had forgotten his wallet they would buy him a pint, and while he was with them they would care for him. He was always safe in their presence. They simply accepted his disability and continued to look after him until I came to collect him. I was very appreciative of their ability to keep him as part of their group for such a long time.

The third group was composed of the two church congregations in Cumbria and Pembrokeshire, with whom he worshipped each week. Brought up in the Welsh valleys to attend church (rather than chapel), he had drifted away from church in the early days of his RAF career but returned when we were posted to Cyprus a year after our marriage in 1965. His Confirmation occurred in his mid-thirties, carried out by the Bishop of Jerusalem, and later it was Adrian who was my greatest supporter as I trained for Ministry in the Church.

Adrian had always helped me in a myriad of ways. He had cared for our boys when I was working, cooked dinners, helped set up Fetes and Fairs, prepared the church for worship on a Sunday, shopped, carried heavy furniture, purchased things needed at the last moment and looked after everything when I was away on conferences. I only had to ask, for him to do whatever was needed. Throughout my time working for the church he was there to support me and act as a back-up, from the moment he cared for our very young children and my disabled mother on my retreat before becoming a full-time Deaconess in Gloucester, to my last job in Cumbria as Team Rector of a group of churches off the Solway Firth. It was something that I missed, but now it was my turn to reciprocate his care.

As Adrian's memory grew worse it was not too obvious within the church context for a long while, but nevertheless eventually I could no longer ask him to help me, for it would get him upset if he couldn't remember for instance, what he had gone to get, or where something needed to go. His loss of memory was not a huge problem on a Sunday during worship. He had known the ritual of the services for years. It was something he had been accustomed to for much of his life. So he knew what to do and where to go. However, a year or two after we moved to Pembrokeshire there came a time when he couldn't follow the service from a prayer book, or find the hymns in a hymn book. Members of the congregation noticed this and took to inviting him to sit with them, before unobtrusively finding the pages he needed, and passing the book to him. They were also ready to guide him to the altar to receive communion, and others would help him back to his seat. Afterwards someone would bring him a cup of coffee, or stay to talk to him for a few moments. This continued even when a large service was held in a nearby church. I was on duty in Tenby one morning. Our friend, Anne, drove him to church and then sat with him. She helped him with books and guided him to the altar to receive communion. However when he left the altar rail he couldn't find his way back to his seat, and she had to search the large congregation to find him, before guiding him back to where he had been sitting.

This kind of care for Adrian from all who attended the church never wavered; they offered whatever he needed. Through to the end of his life members of the congregation would come to visit him, sit alongside him in silence, hold his hand, listen to his odd words, and try and use these to engage in some kind of conversation. If they were women, well he was always up for a smile and a kiss right to the end of his life!

Adrian rarely if ever talked about his faith, but when he did his belief in God never wavered, even when it was obvious to us both what the future would bring. He knew that God loved him, and that this love would continue even when he could no longer remember God. So his visitors and others prayed for him when he could no longer pray himself, and they sung to him, as to a child.

A final person who was to engage with Adrian was a young man living in the village who was willing to take him over to the pub to meet his friends. He would also take Adrian out and about for the day, and even if in later years when Adrian was a little unsure what was going on and who this person was. He never complained about the change in his routine, but was always pleased to get out of the house.

WHAT 'BODY LANGUAGE' CAN TEACH US

All this time I was still trying to find out how I could help Adrian and make his daily life as good as possible. It took a lot of trial and error to find out what worked for him, but each time I found something that helped it felt like a major breakthrough.

I gave this an enormous amount of consideration, and started by watching his body language, to see if this could tell me something when his voice couldn't. I noticed that when he was unhappy his whole posture was less open, his hands could be clenched and his legs crossed. He would sometimes turn his shoulder and whole body away from me or from those who came to see him. His facial expression could also indicate his dissatisfaction, and often he would scowl or frown. Occasionally he would make a muttered comment that was obviously not pleasant, even if we couldn't quite understand him. At other times he would just turn his head away or refuse to give any kind of eye contact.

There was one thing that could confuse me, and that was if Adrian was in pain. If he had a headache or any other part of his body hurt, then he would often show some of the above symptoms, not because he was unhappy or angry, but because he was in some kind of discomfort. Towards the end of his life, when he was unable to speak, the ability to read his body language became of paramount importance.

However, when Adrian was content and pain-free his whole frame would be relaxed and open, his arms and hands tranquil, his body turned towards his visitors and his face peaceful. He would smile and laugh, and he would watch what was going on around him, particularly if this involved children or dogs. He was more likely to give eye contact, although sometimes he would still watch visitors out of the corner of his eye. However, at such times he would also attempt to engage with other people, start conversations or join in exchanges between others.

When I started to really observe Adrian's body language I noticed that there were times when he would begin to mirror my actions or the actions of someone speaking to him. If a visitor smiled, gave him a squeeze or a kiss, or clapped their hands in happiness he would often copy. Sometimes if I nodded, tapped my head, or waved, he would very often do the same thing. This could 'side-track him' and take him out of himself if he were feeling fed-up or unhappy, and a few minutes later he could be in a much better mood.

Over time all of those who visited Adrian regularly began to try and make use of the knowledge being accumulated to help them engage with him as his communications skills diminished. If Adrian became unhappy about something, it would take a while for him to return to his 'sunny self', sometimes up to an hour or so in the early days. In later years it was always best to visit him in the afternoon, because he hated being washed and dressed in the morning, and would be uncommunicative or irritated for some time after this. So going in later was always likely to be better. By using the knowledge gained through observing Adrian we could also hope to keep him at peace with himself and with those around him.

LEARNING FROM THE EXPERT: – THE DEMENTIA PATIENT

At home I began to notice that Adrian's behaviour was often affected by other people. He could be upset by something that was said or done, even if occasionally it was because he didn't understand what was happening. But mostly his behaviour was a reaction to how he was treated (or how he perceived he was treated), so if we were less than patient with him he would react accordingly, or if he felt that he was treated disrespectfully, then he could become angry. His temperament was normally sunny, but occasionally he could be depressed or cross, and it would take some gentle understanding to bring him back to equanimity.

However, as well as learning to understand Adrian's body language I was also beginning to realise that what we thought Adrian needed, might not be what he felt he needed. In the same way that he could misunderstand what we said to him, and react badly, so he could misunderstand what we tried to do for him. When we thought he needed to eat, drink, or bathe, might not agree with what he thought he needed. Consequently, his reactions to us could be different to what we expected. I realised that we needed to think of Adrian as the 'teacher', rather than the 'learner'. We were the ones who were learning, he was the one who knew about dementia. We could only understand this disease by looking at him, and try to put ourselves in his shoes to find out how he felt and discover what he thought he needed.

It was always a balancing act between Adrian's desires and my needs (that is, the tasks that had to be done for him like washing, toileting, and eating as well as caring for my grandchildren who lived with us), and I had to find out how best to walk this difficult plank to achieve the best outcome. I was beginning to appreciate at this time how 'person centred care' worked. I had to put his emotional needs first, and as far as possible the tasks second. Doing this reinforced Adrian's sense of worth making him feel valued, and because he felt valued he was more inclined to allow me to carry out the tasks that I felt had to be done. Later the Nursing Home's attitude to Adrian's care reinforced my belief that taking his emotions into consideration could also make life much easier not just for everyone around him, but even more importantly for Adrian himself.

When he entered the Nursing Home, I would encourage those special people who visited Adrian regularly to be more 'familiar' with him. It was appropriate to give him a kiss (friends as well as family), to look in his eyes and to take his hand, then slowly to start stroke it. Alternatively they could gently stroke or touch his face or head. If this felt far too bold for some visitors they needed to remember that Adrian was not aware of having his personal space invaded, nor did he realise that this was an odd thing for his friends to do. Such social niceties had long since passed out of his consciousness, and they needed to work with his emotional self and not his rational self. For his friends who had sufficient empathy to try and imagine what he might feel about his life, particularly those women who were willing to attempt to understand his emotional needs and who tried out my suggestions, it was the beginning of a fresh and profitable relationship with Adrian.

11. VISITING THE DOCTOR FOR THE SECOND TIME

Adrian's actual diagnosis of dementia took place almost exactly two years after the first abortive attempt to get a diagnosis of his memory problems, and four years after I noticed he was having difficulties. Having seen the Doctor the first time he saw no need to try again and therefore absolutely refused to go to the Surgery, even to have his diabetes measured, unless he was forced to attend. After all the Doctor had told him there was nothing wrong with his memory! The frustration for me was unbelievable, because I knew how far down the dementia road he had travelled. He also didn't have a full diagnosis of his dementia – what kind of dementia was it? Was it Alzheimer's, for instance? If it had been Alzheimers then it might have meant that there was some assistance for him in the early days. This might have slowed the onset of the disease, although by now it would have been too late, for he should have started some kind of medication years ago.

By June of 2013 I felt that it was not only Adrian who needed help. I now wanted assistance, for I was definitely becoming stressed coping with Adrian. I debated once again within myself how I was to deal with this whole situation, not least how I was to inform the Doctor about my concerns over Adrian. If I wrote to the Surgery how was I to get it to the right person and ensure that they actually read it? In the end I once again wrote to the Doctor, not this time a general letter to the practice, but to a specific Doctor that I knew and trusted. I wrote every symptom that Adrian showed and handed it in to the Receptionist at the Surgery, explaining what the letter was about and the need for the Doctor to read it before we came in to see him. The following week I made the appointment, after the same Receptionist assured me the Doctor had read the letter.

The whole plan almost failed, however, when Adrian decided there was no point in going to see the Doctor, and completely refused to attend the Surgery or to get into the car. This was about fifteen minutes before we had to leave. In desperation I told him that I needed to speak to the Doctor myself, and hoped that he would come with me. I was pretty sure he wouldn't remember where we were going by the time we got into the car, or by the time we reached the Surgery.

Even at this traumatic time I was abiding by my rules of not asking Adrian a question, but instead giving him a choice – he could stay at home, or he could join me. Also, I was not prepared to argue with him, there was to be no disagreement on my part. Fifteen minutes before leaving for the Doctors this was extremely difficult, but somehow I managed to keep my cool. My tactics immediately diffused the situation, and because by this time Adrian was accustomed to going everywhere with me, and was always happy to get out of the bungalow he joined me in the car.

As we drove into town I now began to worry whether Adrian would go in to see the Doctor when his name, and not mine, was called? Perhaps he would simply refuse and go back to the car? I had absolutely no idea what would happen. In the end though there was no problem. Adrian entered the room ahead of me and sat down on a chair beside the Doctor's desk. I chose a chair slightly behind him and out of his eye-line. Indeed I suspect that Adrian forgot I was in the room almost immediately.

I had referred to the letter that I had written as we entered the room, and the Doctor glanced at me and nodded. After that I left him to talk to Adrian.

His first question, "And how are you Mr Swain?" elicited an amazing response.

Bearing in mind that questions could often upset him, I rather held my breath, not sure what he would answer. He might well be totally confused and unable to make sense of what he was being asked. However, that was not the case for he immediately gave the Doctor an answer. Words absolutely poured out of him.

"I'm not good," Adrian said immediately, his whole body language changing into one of despondency. "My wife died six months ago. It's very sad. I miss her enormously!"

The Doctor nodded sympathetically and listened to all that Adrian was saying. His eye contact was steadfast and all his attention was on his patient as he allowed him to speak. He exuded compassion, and accordingly Adrian unfolded like a flower. He talked and talked of how awful his life was since his wife had 'died'.

Adrian had never been a person to air his feelings. Since I had first known him he had never spoken of love, except in the letters he had written each day in the first year after we met and were away from one another. He really only showed what he felt for people through his actions. His love for his family, for animals of all kinds, and for children in general, was all shown in this way.

He would cook favourite meals for each of us; give away everything he had to make us happy; and put himself out to help anyone. In this he was very much like his mother, although he refused to believe it. But he would not speak about his feelings, other than a couple of times in his life when he said he thought he was a "very cold person". I could never quite believe that he really thought he was a "cold" person, and it always made me want to laugh, because he was the very antithesis of such a person. Like his mother before him he would do anything he could to help another person.

Yet here in the Doctor's Surgery he was voluble, his emotions were on show for both of us to see. Indeed he was being more open this day than in all the fifty years I had known him.

As the appointment came to an end, I came back to myself. It had been like watching a film. It seemed so far removed from reality that I could barely believe what I was hearing. It was the most terrible shock to discover that Adrian thought that I, his wife, was dead. I felt numbed by the revelation that was being played out in front of me.

Finally the Doctor turned towards me and included me in the conversation. He asked Adrian who I was. There was a pause and Adrian looked at me, before giving an almost seraphic smile.

"She's my Carer," he explained. "She's lovely!"

While I attempted to handle the news that Adrian thought I had died, but yet valued me as someone who looked after him as his official Carer, the Doctor arranged for Adrian to have an appointment to visit the

Memory Clinic at the local hospital in Haverfordwest. They would organise the next stages of his investigation.

After nearly two and a half years, we had finally achieved something. It would take a number of scans to determine that his memory loss was caused by Vascular Dementia. However, his dementia was now an acknowledged fact.

ATTENDING THE DAY CENTRE

The staff at the Memory Clinic had suggested that Adrian attended the Day Centre in Haverfordwest, when there was a space for him. After a few weeks a place became available, and I prepared to send him one day a week. However, the experience of the Day Centre which was near the Memory Clinic was to be a complete disaster. We lived about twenty miles from Haverfordwest and in order to give me a break a courtesy car driven by a volunteer was arranged to take Adrian to the Centre. I was informed I had to have him up and ready to leave fairly early, but by this time I was finding it very hard to wake him up, get him dressed, and give him breakfast. On a normal day I could leave him to wake when he was ready, but now I had to have him up at a specific time. I needed to give him considerable time between waking up, getting him to a chair in the bedroom, helping him to the bathroom, and before he consider eating his breakfast. Further time was needed before he would take his medicine and get dressed.

On the mornings he was due to go to the Day Centre he needed to be ready very early, by 8am or 8.30am. (This could not be helped, since the voluntary car driver had to pick up a number of people, and someone had to be first, depending on the route!) I could not afford to give him all the time that he wanted and was forced to rush him when he wanted to take it slower. I suspect my tension over this was communicated to Adrian, so it meant that both of us were stressed before the car arrived. Things got much worse after this because the courtesy car could arrive an hour or more later than the time I had been given. Because of this I was forced to put Adrian in the small conservatory by the front door, and this was chilly in the winter. He simply could not understand why he had to sit in the cold for so long, effectively outside the bungalow. But if I had left him in the bungalow I would have needed to get his coat on and this could take quite a while if he was unhappy to put it on. I might never have got him to the courtesy car.

Another problem came along fairly quickly. Once Adrian was in the transport he had no idea of where he was going, and he couldn't understand why I was not driving or accompanying him. Neither could he understand why the car had to pick up other strangers on the way. If any of the others had personality problems he struggled to deal with them, and unless he was in the back of the car would try to get out. He appeared terrified that all the things he knew had been taken away from him. I think he was scared that he would never return home. In retrospect it occurred to me that he must have felt he was being kidnapped!

When he did arrive at the Centre he had no idea why he was being greeted by strangers, or why he was there. He apparently felt unable to join in any of the activities on offer that day, and found it difficult to communicate with the other people present. For the first time the staff saw him get angry, if not actually aggressive. He was upset by other confused people around him, did not want to engage with any activity, wasn't impressed with lunch, and then became cross over having to hang around waiting for the car again. Things became so difficult for the staff and for me, that I was forced in the end to stop him attending the Day Centre. This of course meant that I now got no break, and I was still caring for Adrian twenty-four hours a day.

When I thought about it sometime afterwards I realised that the Day Clinic did not offer Adrian the right social experience for him. He had never been one to attend coffee mornings or tea parties unless he was helping me run them in which case he would be working. So attending such a gathering was totally alien to him. The things that did work for him were those he managed to create for himself, for instance at the local pub. The forced social scene at the Day Centre where everyone had many of the same kind of difficulties, simply didn't work for Adrian. Obviously the clients had no concept of 'person centred' care, and the staff seemed to be too overworked to put such a philosophy in place. To be fair the Centre was trying to offer activities for people at different stages of their dementia journey, so some of the things offered were simply not appropriate for Adrian. Added to this the clients seemed to be a shifting population, so each week there might be different people present. I suspect this whole system would work much better if the Centre had been more local and there were people present whom

Adrian knew. I am sure that limited finances would not have allowed for this possibility though.

Perhaps because the Day Centre was alongside the Memory Clinic Adrian seemed to link the two different places together in his mind. So he saw the Centre as somewhere that would make an assessment of his capabilities. The activities offered were not seen as games. Adrian saw them as tests. This, together with the inability to get out of the building or to return home, meant he became very frustrated and angry. So the next week when the car came, things became even worse. He obviously still had some residual memory of the previous week at this time.

Adrian's late diagnoses of vascular dementia, his unhappiness at attending the Day Centre, and the fact that I didn't want to go ahead with respite care, meant that the whole care package simply resolved back onto me. Within a few months I was to take over full-time care of my two young grandchildren. The future began to look a little bleak for all of us.

12. THE LAST TWO YEARS AT HOME

In December of 2013 six months after Adrian was diagnosed with dementia our two grandchildren, aged nine and eleven years joined us from Peru. While their father completed a post-graduate teaching certificate at Aberystwyth University and their mother awaited her visa, the two children came to live with us. Adrian and I picked up D___ and the grandchildren from Heathrow Airport before travelling back to Pembrokeshire. Adrian was quiet on the way back though happy to speak to the children. I assumed he knew they were his grandchildren, but he was good at hiding his thoughts sometimes, so it was difficult to tell. He might have thought they were some children of a friend, especially as Adrian had failed to recognise our younger son, K___ a few weeks earlier. In fact I never did discover if Adrian knew the children were his grandchildren. He never questioned their presence in our home, but simply accepted them.

Although the children spoke very little English after years of living in Peru, they did understand quite a lot of the language. Thrown instantly into the local Primary School, where they had to learn Welsh as well as English, they somehow coped amazingly well and were quickly at home in Pembrokeshire.

Adrian certainly enjoyed the presence of the children and loved their company, although the addition of two young children in a small bungalow, sleeping in the bedroom next to ours and with their father sleeping on a sofa bed in the living room at weekends, was not very easy. However I valued having more hands and eyes to help keep an unobtrusive watch over Adrian, and I loved having their happy voices around the bungalow.

As the weeks went by I became accustomed to getting up at 6.30 am in the morning, and realised how lazy we had become after our retirement. The morning was always a rush – waking up the children, preparing breakfast, getting them ready for the day (with the usual complaint from our grandson that he had to do his homework) and then driving them to school. I would leave Adrian in bed until I had taken them down to the village school, before returning to help him get washed and dressed, and try to entice him to eat his breakfast and take his tablets. In the afternoon we would both go and pick them up from school, and the homework merry-go-round would start all over again.

More signs of dementia were beginning to show in Adrian now. He had always cooked the Christmas dinner, and would be up at the crack of dawn on Christmas day to put the turkey in the oven. While I was out taking church services he would work on the dinner and we were always treated to a beautifully cooked meal at 1 o'clock on the dot. However, things began to change. The previous year we noticed that the sprouts were missing from our meal! We all loved sprouts and there was a moan all around the table. Adrian did not seem the slightest bit concerned and made no excuse about why they were missing. In fact he ignored the whole subject. He appeared to have no empathy with us over the missing sprouts, and we gave up trying to share our concern with him, and decided to have the sprouts another day.

However, this Christmas things got worse. It was going to be a very special time because the grandchildren had joined us, but halfway through the morning we discovered that the turkey wasn't cooking. Adrian simply said "The oven hasn't come on!" Since we had experienced problems with the oven-timer in the past, I thought no more about it. We just had a later dinner that day. In retrospect, it was obvious that Adrian had lost control over the cooker and was unable to use it properly. However, at the time I took his comments at face value, and thought no more about it, although K___ had already made the right conclusion about the event.

In the New Year we were visited by two Social Workers. They attempted to convince me that I needed help, but I found the need to apply for a CRB check to care for my husband totally offensive. I was actually angry that someone would want to check my credentials to see if I could look after Adrian. We had spent forty-odd years caring for each other! To be fair the thinking was that I needed to be checked in order to apply for funding to employ a Carer. I knew I was probably being irrational, but the whole procedure felt intrusive and unnecessary. In the end I decided I would continue to look after Adrian as well as the grandchildren on my own for as long as I possibly could, and not apply for funding to employ someone else.

This year brought some odd occurrences. Adrian decided to put his money into the washing machine, both his wallet and the coins in his pocket. I found myself drying notes on all the radiators, which perplexed him as he had forgotten what he'd done.

These days his interest in money grew. Our friend Jane sat with Adrian in church one Sunday and watched as he got his money out of his suit pocket (where I had put it) for the collection. Having got it where he wanted it she said he then spent most of the service moving it around to all of his other pockets. She said she tried to keep track of which pocket it was in, but when the collection plate came round it had disappeared. We found it after the service tucked up his sleeve!

BUYING SHOES

Then in June I decided that I had to sort out Adrian's shoes. He had spent months fidgeting with them, as though they were uncomfortable or felt strange to him. He was constantly undoing the laces and trying to do them up again. If he couldn't manage this he just got cross with them. Since his ability to retie the shoe laces was disappearing, I decided he needed some shoes that had a different kind of fastening, and our grandson kindly showed Adrian his new shoes that used a Velcro fastening. Adrian had seen such shoes before when our own lads had been much younger, but he hadn't realised that adult's shoes could have such fastenings. However, he nodded happily, and we went into Haverfordwest to see what we could find. I was determined to buy him some really good quality shoes and so we went into Clark's shoe-shop. In the event the assistant in the shop was very helpful, seeming to have all the time in the world to help us.

All his life Adrian had bought a size ten shoe, but it occurred to me that it might be a good idea to have his feet measured first. As he was losing weight I wondered if his foot size had changed. The resulting fiasco deserved to be put on television.

I explained to the shop assistant that my husband had dementia, and that I wanted his feet measured. The place was fairly empty and she led us to the back of the shop. Adrian took off his shoes and stood looking somewhat bewildered among the children's shoes. He obviously could not understand why he was in the children's section of the shop. I encouraged him to stand on the machine, but he was nervous about doing so, thinking he would fall. I took off my shoes and showed him what I meant. He just stared blankly at me. Finally he popped a toe on the machine for a second and then withdrew it. I encouraged him to try again!

The scenario continued for some time, as he popped a toe in and then out of the machine. It was like a dance. He seemed to enjoy doing it, but by this time we had other people watching. They began to suggest how we might achieve success.

"Try having your own foot scanned!" said one lady.

I did so. Adrian looked on with interest but made no move to comply.

"Now you, AD," I said encouragingly.

He smiled sweetly at me. I was beginning to learn that a sweet smile but no verbal response meant he didn't know what I was saying but was trying to be helpful.

"Put your foot in the machine so it can scan your foot!" I encouraged.

Adrian nodded slowly, still smiling, but didn't move.

The assistant now spoke, suddenly seeming to understand what might be needed. "Can you put your foot in here, for me?" she asked gently as though talking to a small child (which of course she was very accustomed to doing). She looked straight into his eyes and smiled at him supportively.

Suddenly Adrian answered. "Yes" and moved to comply.

As simple as that, one foot went into the machine and the assistant was able to measure the width and length of his foot. Then the other foot was measured.

The remarkable discovery made that day was that he had always worn the wrong size shoes. He was actually a size eight but had a very wide foot. Presumably he had worn a size ten for the whole of his life in order to give himself a wider shoe. I remembered that he had always had trouble with his RAF shoes which had caused him great pain. He would end up with raw feet, and subsequently a number of corns.

Adrian had certainly never had his feet measured before. In fact it had never occurred to me that either of us could ask to have such a check. Pleased at having established the correct size, I now chose two leather shoes, similar to the style he always chose, but this time with strong Velcro fastenings. His feet should be much more comfortable in the future, all thanks to the thoughtful understanding of the assistant. Indeed the shoes were so comfortable that he wore a pair of them out of the shop that day.

A STRANGE HABIT DEVELOPS

During this year Adrian developed a strange habit that I called 'butterfly catching'. He would try to grab invisible things in the air. It was as though he was trying to catch butterflies or feathers floating down from the sky. He would lean forward and seemingly gently pluck something out of the air with his hand. I would respond by holding out my hand, and he would place the invisible item that he had 'caught' into my palm. Often I would comment on the beauty or size of the object he had placed there, before pretending to put it somewhere safe. It was always important to engage with his 'story' whatever it was, and to go along with the pretence. After he had given it to me he would watch in contentment as I placed the imaginary item somewhere safe.

There was one massive difficulty with this habit, though, for sometimes Adrian would bend over to catch the invisible item just before it touched the carpet. Often he would completely topple onto the floor. Alternately he would bring his head back up again so sharply, that he would hit his head on any nearby table or chair. We would have to watch him even more closely I thought.

THE DIFFICULTY OF HAVING HEALTH CHECKS

Other changes that occurred at this time concerned various health checks that Adrian needed. As a diabetic Adrian was due an annual check-up, which included having his eyes screened. It was a simple test that both of us as diabetics were accustomed to receiving. First some drops were put into the eyes, and then after fifteen minutes or so, once the pupils had enlarged, a series of pictures would be taken of the back of his eyes. Adrian was required to put his chin onto a rest and to hold his head still, while following the operator's instructions to "Look at the white light!" or "Look at the red light". There was some disagreement this year over whether I would be allowed into the room as his Carer to help Adrian. However, I pointed out that unless I entered the room he wouldn't be able to comply with the instructions from the clinician. Finally it was agreed I could help.

As Adrian was asked to look at the red or white light, with one eye or the other, I tapped the right or left side of his head, wherever the light appeared, and he was able to move his eyes to the correct direction. I asked the technician what would happen if Adrian couldn't follow the light with his eyes.

"We'd be unable to do the test," he said, seemingly totally uninterested in the fact that it might affect Adrian's future eyesight. He obviously didn't see it as part of his job to have empathy with his patient or Carer.

I was appalled at the technician's words at the time, but then forgot about them over the next few months until the autumn, when we went to the Nurse for our flu jabs. We both went into the Surgery together, and I had my jab first. Adrian hesitated, and it looked as though he was going to refuse to have the flu jab. I had a little struggle to get him to roll up his sleeve, but then after a moment's hesitation Adrian allowed the Nurse to put the needle into his arm. I remembered the conversation with the eye technician earlier in the year, and realised that the outcome at the Surgery would have been the same if I had not led the way, and if he was unable to co-operate. Another year the whole scenario might be different.

I found myself thinking about the whole subject of health services that might not be accessed by dementia patients. I was beginning to realise that someone with dementia could end up in a situation where they would no longer have most of the medical health checks that the rest of us take for granted. What would happen if Adrian had toothache but couldn't keep his mouth open or allow the Dentist to work on his mouth, or suppose he needed a hearing check which would depend totally on his responding to sounds produced in his ears. Then there was his two-monthly Podiatrist appointment which helped keep the soles of his feet free of seed-corns, how would this work? The last time she had come we had found it extremely difficult to persuade Adrian to let her work on his feet despite the fact that he knew her well and was attracted to her lovely Irish accent which brought back many memories of his three years in Northern Ireland. I had visions of the corns recurring on his feet.

The whole question of knowing how to understand if someone was in pain, if they couldn't communicate what was wrong, concerned me enormously. It was the same difficulty that must occur with very young children, I realised. If Adrian had a stomach ache how would we know? It was less concerning if it were a pain in an arm or a leg, because he would probably hold the limb in a different way, or not use it. I noticed in months to come that he would hold his head with one hand and frown when the television was too noisy or he was too near it, and presumably he had a headache.

Similarly how would he communicate his difficulty over putting in his false tooth? Adrian had lost a front tooth when playing rugby as a hooker while a young man, and amazingly the Dentist at the time had decided the space was too small so he had taken another perfectly good tooth out, and given him a single tooth on a plate. Adrian was always very conscious about this space in the front of his mouth and put the false tooth into his mouth immediately after putting on his glasses first thing in the morning. To be fair I could ignore the tooth pretty soon, since once he entered the Nursing Home it instantly disappeared, and as for his perfectly good state-of-the-art hearing aid, well he never wore it complaining that it made everything too loud. But all the other health checks were important. If he couldn't undergo these, his health would be affected, and he might end up in pain.

My conclusions about Adrian's general health and the need for any services from the professionals led to one simple conclusion. If a person is not compliant or cannot answer questions then none of these systems can be accessed or used. It made me sad and angry at the same time, for it meant that anyone with dementia would always be treated as a second-class citizen with regard to their health, and the last years of their life might be made far more difficult for them and their Carers.

FAVOURITE TELEVISION PROGRAMMES ARE IGNORED

During the spring and summer of the next year another change to Adrian began to affect us all. It started in a fairly innocuous way with him losing interest in most television programmes. I had noticed that programmes on television which Adrian had watched for years were no longer as interesting to him now. In the past I would record anything that I knew appealed to him, so I could put it on when he began to look bored. Now some of these were proving to have no interest for him.

Born in Wales, but moving to Staffordshire when he was a teenager, Adrian had lost his Welsh accent overnight after a keen English teacher made the mistake of telling the boys in his class they should listen to Adrian's wonderful Welsh accent. The same teacher was obviously trying to encourage him as a newcomer, but constantly asking a fifteen year old to read aloud was the last way to do this. As a result Adrian perfected an English accent as quickly as possible, except for the times when he had to say "year" or "ear" which always came out as pure Welsh. Indeed when I first met him at RAF Hereford in 1964 I thought he was English! I certainly had a shock when I met his parents – I could hardly understand what they were saying because of their strong Welsh accents, and I was always having to say, "Pardon?" Half the time I just had to guess what they were saying. It took years before I could easily understand them.

Because of his early upbringing and his national identity though, Adrian had always been a rugby fan. He had played the game when he was younger at school, as well as when he first joined the RAF. If the national team played it was always a special occasion and we would have a great afternoon. He would get in the beer and friends would come round. If either of his sons were at home this would make it an even more festive afternoon. As an adult he always supported England, the one exception was when Wales played England, and then he would switch allegiances. His heart was still with Wales, even though he had lived all his life, except for his childhood, in England.

Now though I would put on the television and tell him that there was an international rugby match about to start. To my amazement after a few moments of watching the match he would wander away and ignore the game. Even the playing of the national anthem or the singing of the well-known songs and hymns before the game would spark no response. It had been so much a part of his whole life that I felt saddened at his lack of interest.

Another favourite television programme had always been Formula One racing, which he had watched week after week in the season, but the same thing was to happen with this. He would lose interest after a few moments, wander away, and I would eventually turn off the television.

Confusion

However, if there were programmes that Adrian no longer watched at this time, a problem occurred regarding the television that was completely bizarre. I loved to watch a number of detective programmes, including Agatha Christie's 'Miss Marple' and 'Midsummer Murders'. Adrian would join me in the evening and we'd endeavour to work out the identity of the murderer. We enjoyed ourselves, laughing at the number of people who would be killed, just outside a house, by a hedge and in the darkness of the evening. Neither of us were very good at spotting the murderer, but we enjoyed trying to turn detective.

As Adrian's dementia progressed though, I was forced to change our habit of watching such programmes. One night our grandson came running into the kitchen where I had momentarily gone.

He was very agitated. "Adrian thinks soldiers with guns are coming after him!" he whispered looking back, rather worried that Adrian might have followed him.

As a serviceman Adrian had been trained to use guns, and each year had to do a firearms handling course right up until he left the RAF when he was fifty-five years old. On entering the living room I found him looking anxiously out of the window. He was half hidden behind a curtain, peering round the edge of it. Since the window only looked onto a fence between us and the next door neighbour, there was actually little to see, but he was obviously very nervous.

"There's soldiers out there," he said worriedly.

Unobtrusively I turned off the television where he had been watching a detective programme with soldiers in it, and went into reassurance mode, remembering not to disagree with him.

"They're gone now, I said. "They're probably from the camp down the road - just checking out the area to keep us all safe!"

He turned and looked at me for a second giving me a very straight look, and I wasn't sure whether he would accept my matter of fact assurance, or fleetingly would realise that what I was saying made no sense - in which case I would certainly get short shrift from him. I waited with bated breath to see what he would say.

However, he simply nodded and went to sit down again. The moment had passed, and he had obviously forgotten the incident. I put the television back on again, this time to something less controversial, and went into the kitchen to explain the whole affair to our grandson who had been upset by what had happened. After some considerable discussion when I tried to make him understand how Adrian felt about guns and their use, he agreed that he would not play with his own extensive collection of plastic guns (kept behind the sofa) when Adrian was around. This was very hard for him since he loved playing imaginary war games. A compromise was finally reached. He would play with his guns in the back garden, out of sight of his grandfather.

After a number of similar incidents I made sure that we only watched Cooking, Holiday, Housing or Archaeology programmes on the television. Over the next six months I began to long for something a little meatier to watch as Adrian began to continually confuse drama programmes with reality. Our grandson had to make sure that he played his computer games out of sight of his grandfather as well, and we all began to watch much more Children's Television. It might have been boring for the rest of the family, but it allowed Adrian to be at peace.

Another subject I needed to handle with the children concerned Adrian's growing confusion, and the struggle he was having with reality. Our granddaughter was particularly helpful at this time. She took all Adrian's oddities in her stride and would give him a cuddle or speak gently to him, and then take him by the hand if he looked worried or concerned about anything. She never disagreed with him, but would enter his subject of conversation and agree with him. She would also make sure she watched programmes that didn't cause him any difficulty. I think he imagined he was watching them for her sake. As a girl who loved artwork she would encourage him to do some drawing. In retrospect I rather wished I had given him one of the adult-colouring books. He might have enjoyed doing that.

PROBLEMS WHILE WAITING AT THE HOSPITAL

As a grandparent, I found living with two young children a joy. Each day was different to the one before. One moment I was helping them with their homework which I hadn't done for many years, and struggling to work out math's programmes or understand their projects, and the next moment I would be making Lego models. Adrian gained pleasure out of the children's company, but nevertheless their advent in our lives brought with it some unexpected consequences. One of these occurred on a sunny Sunday evening in summer. I was cooking a roast dinner and was about to serve up the meal, when the door-bell went.

Standing outside the door was a strange man accompanied by our grandson, the latter looking rather wan faced and obviously in pain. He had only just been allowed to ride his bike around a small estate over the road, and I had promised his mother that no harm would come to him only that previous night. He had been told to return at a specific time for dinner. Well he was back, but had obviously come off his bike. Apparently he tried to do a 'wheelie' up the curb, with the result that he fell over the handlebars, and had to be rescued by a kind neighbour. All this is on the first week of the summer holiday!

My heart sank at what I was going to say to his parents. However forgetting that, I took one look at the wounded rider, and realised he had broken his arm. Shouting to the others, "In the car, everyone!" I quickly turned off the cooker leaving our Sunday roast dinner to go to ruin and grabbed the keys, before finding a piece of cloth to tie his arm to his body and a cushion to rest it on. Then I shepherded the whole family into the car and took off, driving the twenty miles to the Hospital.

For the first few miles I was concerned with driving fairly slowly so that our grandson didn't suffer any more pain than was necessary when we were forced to go over any bumps. But after a while things settled down and we made good time. Adrian always sat in the front seat of the car, but this night I had been forced to put our grandson where I could see him. Suddenly there was a rather plaintive voice from the back seat.

"Where are we going?" asked Adrian, in total confusion as to what was happening.

I suddenly realised that he had been unable to 'read the situation', and perhaps had not heard the conversation about having to rush to the Hospital. I quickly put him in the picture, not knowing if he really understood what I was saying, but unable to think more carefully as I drove the car. Normally I would look Adrian in the face when I talked to him, using eye contact to reinforce what I was saying, but in this instance it was impossible.

This was only the beginning of the problems that were to occur that night. My attention was necessarily taken up with our grandson when we reached the hospital and I had to leave his older sister to cope with Adrian while I took the patient into triage. I returned after we had seen a Nurse and were waiting for an X-ray, to find our eleven year old granddaughter wandering around in the, by now chilly and dark night, outside the hospital following her grandfather wherever he went. Adrian had not felt he could obey a young girl (probably not knowing who she was) and stay inside the Accident and Emergency Department. As far as he was concerned, I had disappeared and he was solely concerned with the fact that I had vanished. He simply didn't know where I had gone. He just knew he needed to find me, and so went outside to do just that.

Noticing a separate room for children, overlooked by the Receptionist, I wished someone had told them they needed such a room for dementia patients. I rescued Adrian and settled everyone down in the waiting room again, making sure they could see the television which had on a current affairs programme. However, the situation was to get worse when we went through to the X-Ray department and then finally the Plaster room. Halfway through trying to calm my grandson I periodically needed to return and check on my husband. It was a very difficult evening.

In retrospect I should have given Adrian some 'clue' as to where I had gone when I had left him and how long I would be, in the same way that I did at home. Perhaps this couldn't have been the tray and teapot that I used at home, but it could have been something similar to the physical movement I made to indicate that I was going to the toilet (ie crossing my legs!) or I could waved to him, telling him where I was going, and pretend I was washing my hands. He would always accepted these indications and nod acceptingly before going back to whatever was interesting him at the time, content that he knew where I was going. In the Hospital, I should have stood beside our grandson and mimed washing my hands, while telling him where I was going. He would have assumed that I was taking our grandson to find the toilet, and hopefully would have been content to stay in the waiting room. Unfortunately my concern was with our grandson that night and not my husband, so I took my eye of the ball for a moment.

By the time we left the Hospital some four hours later we were all starving, and Adrian was actually complaining that he was hungry, which since his appetite was never good at this time, was great. In the wilds of rural Pembrokeshire on the particular journey we were making there was nowhere open at that time of night to purchase food. Finally we returned home and reheated the dinner we had left so suddenly earlier that evening. By eleven o'clock we were all sitting down to a roast meal.

A few weeks later we followed up the first Hospital appointment with another, and travelled to Carmarthen to attend the Fracture Clinic. This proved to be an even greater challenge. The waiting room was almost full, holding dozens of people attending a number of different clinics. I couldn't find somewhere for us all to sit or even stand together, and I had to guide Adrian around people's feet and their pushchairs. He couldn't see the obstacles, and it took some time to find a seat and then we were nowhere near the grandchildren. Again, I had to leave Adrian in the waiting room. Luckily we were not away for long, but my heart was in my mouth the whole time I was away from him.

On leaving I did ask the receptionist if there had been somewhere I could have left Adrian.

"Oh yes, there's a small room down the corridor. You could have left him in there!" she answered cheerfully.

I glanced in the room and noticed that it wasn't possible to lock it ('health and safety rules' obviously), so Adrian would simply have walked out. The need for a 'safe space' for vulnerable adults, exactly like the one provided for children, seemed to have escaped the Hospital's attention.

I needed to give Adrian most of my attention at this time. Usually I could balance things within the home, especially with help from the children who would warn me if Adrian needed me. He was particular close to our granddaughter and would listen to her most of the time. It was lovely to remember that when she had been a toddler Adrian had spent hours reading to her or playing with her and now she returned the favour.

After Adrian's diagnosis of dementia I saw the Social Worker at Pembroke Dock Hospital to discuss future plans for Adrian as I mentioned earlier, and to explore what might be put in place to help him and also the whole family. Subsequently the promised Occupational Therapist came to look at putting in handles to help with Adrian's balance getting in and out of the house, as well as aids for the bathroom. He was to spend the next week or two intrigued by the red circular labels around the house – marks to show where the contractor would put grab handles.

Adrian also saw a Psychiatric Social Worker, and then after that he attended the Memory Clinic in Haverfordwest again. While I talked with a nurse he undertook some simple tests concerned with spatial awareness and memory. It was agreed that he had regressed enormously since the previous year. He was now unable to copy any shapes, or to work out any simple problems.

CHANGE OF TEMPERAMENT

In mid-August our friends Mark and Jane came to stay for a couple of weeks in August. We had known them for many years, and every year they would spend a week or two with us. As I have mentioned earlier Jane had been my parish secretary. Her husband, Mark, was a wonderful handyman. He had built the fence to keep the dogs in, and done many other jobs over the last few years. The two of them would sleep in the spare room, or else in the caravan outside the bungalow, or even in a tent in the garden depending on how many people were staying. It was lovely to see them, but on their first evening with us, just as we were all settling down to watch television with a can of beer or a glass of wine, Adrian turned to Mark and glared at him.

"When are you going home?" he asked somewhat truculently.

This was no question about how long was their holiday. He simply had not recognised them and thought this strange handyman was staying rather too late for his liking. We gently reminded him that they had come for a short holiday, and he said no more.

This was the beginning of the problem that Adrian was to have with men. He found it much easier to identify with women, and was happy to joke with them, blow kisses, and generally enjoy their company. With men he would stare at them suspiciously, often out of the corner of his eye, rarely talking to them, unless it was to be rude to them. This applied to both our sons as well as other men.

Many people suffering from dementia undergo great changes in their personality, becoming violent, or alternatively withdrawn. Even the most peaceful man or woman can turn into a raging virago without any warning. One of the reasons why sufferers are sometimes put into a Home is because their family can no longer cope with their change of temperament. Loved ones who have never said 'boo to a goose' can suddenly lash out, hitting family members, or screaming and shouting at them with no warning. They can become a danger to themselves, and certainly to those around them. However Adrian was usually a calm and measured man, rarely at this time losing his cool, even if he struggled with other men or with his grandson.

In the end I had to keep the latter away from Adrian, for he would continually tell off the ten year old, while being charming to his twelve year old sister. It was also during this period that he failed to recognise our son D___, and if he referred to him at all it was as a child. To him our children were boys, not men in their thirties. This probably meant that he had no knowledge of who the grandchildren were, but simply accepted their presence in the house as children who needed somewhere to live.

However, in the September of this year when our son K___ got married Adrian reverted for the afternoon to the Adrian of old. There were only nine of us at the wedding (both of our sons in fact chose to have small intimate weddings), which I conducted at our local parish church. Adrian seemed to thoroughly enjoy the whole experience. D___ and his wife J___ had chosen a small family wedding at the country church beside our Rectory some years previously, and it was obvious that Adrian now found K___'s wedding at our local church in Pembrokeshire equally natural. He was accustomed to attending this church each Sunday and felt completely at home there. Because of the small number of us at the wedding, I could make the service work for all of us including Adrian. As the grandchildren sang a surprise anthem for the newlyweds Adrian stood alongside them. In the photographs afterwards he is relaxed and attentive, and at the reception he is seen smiling and joking with family members.

DELUSIONS AND OTHER PROBLEMS

Over the autumn though, as his dementia became worse, other things began to happen. He had been having difficulties with his sight – not being able to see items on his dinner plate, and there was an incident in a café where he was unable to place a white cup onto the holder on the white saucer, so the coffee was spilt across the table and floor. I later learnt that white is a poor background colour for those with dementia, and I changed his dinner plate to a beautiful blue one. Another difficulty with his eyesight occurred over the carpet clips in the house. Adrian began to believe that these were steps.

He also began having constant delusions. He would see animals or children that were not there in the corner of room, which would upset all of us and in particular our grandchildren.

At other times he would talk to his sons as friends, and refer to his sons as though they were still children instead of adults in their thirties. He had never spoken to people using their name (indeed there were times that I wondered if I had lost my name), and this became useful for him when he was unsure who people really were. However it also became difficult for those around him as none of us had any idea whom he thought he was addressing.

In the village pub one night his sons endeavoured to start a conversation that would include Adrian, so they began to talk about Cyprus. Sure enough he expanded on his experiences in Cyprus. We had lived there for three years, the year after we were married in 1965, some forty-five years previously, when Adrian had been posted there while he was in the RAF. However he now insisted that he had lived in Cyprus a couple of years earlier. It would have been best to ignore this, since everyone knew this was untrue, and Adrian did not react well to disagreement. Unfortunately K___ pointed out to his father that Adrian had lived there years before he had actually been born. However, Adrian would not have it, and insisted that he had lived in Cyprus just two or three years previously. He appeared to ignore everything that was being said, and became irrationally angry, refusing to listen to either of his sons in the end. In retrospect I think Adrian was muddling two holidays in Cyprus with the longer period that we had lived there.

During the winter Adrian developed some nervousness about sitting down. There were hilarious moments which seemed to go on for hours instead of minutes, as first one hand was placed on the arm of a chair, only to have it removed when the second hand found the opposite arm. Finally becoming confident that he was safe however he would collapse into the chair with relief.

By early January 2015 this trouble with sitting down had got much worse, and he was finding it very difficult to sit in a chair, even with help. He spent a lot of time in our bedroom in a chair by the window. The chair did have good arm support for him to push upwards in order to stand or to sit, but I had to be with him when he wanted to move. He was also sleeping badly, and would wake in the middle of the night. Often he would sleep in very late in the morning. However I was unable to do this as I had to take our grandson to school in the morning, and make sure our granddaughter had breakfast and got onto the High School bus. Consequently I was getting up very early, going to bed late, and then being woken up during the night when Adrian wanted to wander around the house.

By the last day of January in the New Year I had given in and contacted the Social Worker. With their help I decided to apply for money to pay for a Carer for Adrian. This would only give me a break for a few hours a week, but at least it would enable me to get away to do shopping, go to the bank or have my hair done. So I finally took Adrian into Haverfordwest with me to present the CRB forms to County Hall for checking, so that I could employ someone to look after Adrian.

Two days later a Carer suggested by the Social Worker came to meet Adrian to begin to get to know him. She seemed to be able to handle him well, talking with him and engaging him in conversation. I left her with Adrian while I made a cup of tea, and he didn't follow me into the kitchen. After another ten minutes I went next door for a few minutes to talk with my neighbour. When I returned all seemed well, and we arranged for the Carer to come back the following week when I could take some more time off.

That week Adrian saw the Occupational Therapist who felt that he was depressed. A few days later I collected new medication to combat the depression. A week later however he was very ill with a bladder infection. Suddenly he could no longer use the toilet, and after two weeks of trying to help him get up at night to go to the bathroom, followed by one night when he had got up twenty-seven times to walk down the corridor (but in most cases never made it to the bedroom door, and for the rest of the time never reached the bathroom), I knew I was in serious trouble. I could no longer leave him to take our grandson to school, but worse than that I couldn't get Adrian dressed and toileted, or cleaned. He would not let me help, and neither could he do it himself.

Within twenty-four hours the District Nurse and the Social Worker arrived, the former to give him some treatment for his infection, and the latter bringing with her Sue the owner of a nearby Nursing Home. An hour later I had agreed that Adrian should go into the Home for some respite care. I had managed to wait eighteen months from the first time that respite care was suggested, but knew I could continue no more. Three days after he had gone into the Home for a few days respite I had come to my senses and agreed that my lovely husband should remain permanently to be cared for by professional staff.

13. THE NURSING HOME

The Nursing Home that had been suggested for Adrian was a beautiful place in the countryside on the edge of a large village, about half-an-hour's drive away. The main house was a Georgian building with extending arms, in secluded grounds surrounded by fields and woods. On a slight rise it was possible to see a considerable distance across the countryside from the large rear lounge with its picture windows. Every resident had their own room, and they were able to make it into a comfortable place for themselves. The public rooms and corridors were filled with pictures and objects to help stimulate the resident's minds - items on cooking, on gardening, and on different countries around the world. The whole place was light, open and inviting.

Families and friends were welcome to visit the Home at any time, and there was always someone to make them a drink. In the afternoon residents might as easily be offered a beer as a cup of tea. But perhaps the greatest thing for me was the fact that despite having many incontinent dementia residents the home smelt sweet and fresh. My past knowledge of residential homes in many parishes over many years had not led me to expect this.

The Nursing Home must have come as a considerable shock to Adrian. To be torn from his own home and family and placed somewhere with twenty or more strange residents and unknown Carers, would not have been a good experience. He never spoke about how he felt over the move to the Home, but then Adrian had hardly ever opened his heart to tell anyone about his feelings. For the past couple of years I had only been able to tell how he felt through his body language and his actions, and this was particularly so for the last twenty months of his life at the Nursing Home.

I stayed away from the Nursing Home for ten days on the advice of the staff, allowing him to settle in and get used to the change of environment. When I did call I found him little different. He didn't rail at me for placing him in the Home, neither did he complain about anything. The staff said he was fine, though he didn't like being washed or changed. A few weeks later I was outside the Home when I heard the most terrible screaming and shouting. As far away as I was (that is, two corridors and about three room away, in the centre of the complex), I could tell it was Adrian. I learnt afterwards that it took three or even four members of staff to change him for the first few months, and through to his death two or three Carers could still be involved in this task.

Thinking this over I realised that Adrian had never been cleaned or dressed by any person since he was a child. He was essentially a very private man, and he couldn't understand why people were 'interfering' with him. He seemed to think they were prostitutes, and he made his anger felt very strongly. I am not sure he ever got used to this. In the last few weeks of his life one Carer said "He's too compliant!" We were all sad at this evidence of his failing health.

It was interesting that over the first few months staff kept saying to me "How did you manage to look after Adrian for so long?" In their opinion I had done this for far too long, especially when I told them that I was looking after my grandchildren as well. It did my self-esteem wonders to be told this. In the meantime my estimation of the staff went up enormously at the way they dealt with Adrian, with compassion and patience. In the times I was in the Home I never once heard anything but kindness given to any resident, no matter what provocation occurred.

The Nursing Home's philosophy

One of the earliest things I discovered about the Home concerned its philosophy. Before Adrian went into the Nursing Home Sue, the owner, mentioned that they were influenced by David Sheard the founder of 'Dementia Care Matters', a strategy for those working with dementia sufferers as well as their Carers. She said they were "working towards putting his philosophy in place". They had not yet achieved all that was possible, but were heavily influenced by his thinking. Like other such philosophies David Sheard's work puts compassion back into the whole processing of caring for someone. It encourages those who care for residents to move from 'task centred care' to 'person centred care', and to take their emotional as well as their physical needs into account.

A task-centred approach to care puts the physical needs of feeding, toileting, cleaning, dressing, and putting residents to bed (that is the things that must be done each day), first. These are all extremely important, but they can encourage a tick-box mentality that checks for instance, whether all the residents have been fed, or put to bed. It does not necessarily satisfy the resident's emotional needs.

A person-centred approach will still ensure that the physical needs are catered for, but it allows for more flexibility than the tick-box approach. If a resident wants to stay longer in bed in the morning because their night had been disrupted, this would be considered fine. If someone's appetite is poor, a Carer might go and find food that would interest them. Carers are prepared to sit and comfort residents if they are upset, they will spend time talking with them, or engage in song or dance with them. The physical tasks will still get done, but the Carer is driven as much by the emotional demands of the residents as their physical demands.

Despite often being short of staff, the Home found time to try and understand the emotional needs of each person in the Home. Some Carers understood the ethos better than others, but nevertheless there was a real effort to try and make the policy work. Perhaps the foundation stone for this was the emphasis on the Nursing Home being the residents 'home'.

In our own homes we have freedom to make choices about what we do – where we move, or sit, or eat and on when we get up or go to bed. We have likes and dislikes and these can be acceptable to others. Not everyone will want a sweet pudding, or a cup of tea. Others will want no pudding, but would like a hot chocolate or a beer. In our own homes we know who will take sugar in their coffee, and who dislikes milk in tea. These are the small things that make a home a home!

Rules were certainly present in the Nursing Home, but were there to be adapted to meet the needs of each resident. The more astute staff were able to carry out tasks in a way that met the emotional needs of their residents. A task-centred approach to getting residents out of bed would mean starting at one end of a corridor and proceeding down the corridor in an orderly fashion, whether residents were ready to get up or not. An emotional-centred approach decides who are the early-birds and who are not, and thinks about whether a resident might have been up half the night or slept since early evening.

LIFE IN THE HOME

During the first few weeks of visiting the Nursing Home I was impressed with what I saw. Adrian was sitting at a table in the dining room to eat his meals, walking down the corridors on his own, and going into different lounges. In good weather he was going out onto the terrace. He seemed to have found a measure of freedom in the Home. The first time I called in I actually found Adrian jiving with Sue the owner of the Home, and after a moment he danced with me. He was thoroughly enjoying himself. He loved listening to music of an era that appealed to him. All too often there is a belief that the elderly all want to hear war-time songs, but for many it is the rock-an-roll era that appeals. The Home had made an effort to include both kinds of music. He was often to be found watching videos (so keeping residents away from any television programmes that might worry them), and if this dissatisfied him he would walk away to another lounge, just as he would have done in the bungalow.

The Nursing Home was punctilious in celebrating birthdays and anniversaries as they occurred. If residents didn't always know what they were celebrating, the party atmosphere was appreciated. There was always a lot of cake on offer (after all it's a constant battle to keep the weight of each resident up to scratch!). Families, whether small or large, were always welcome at these events, and the Home was a happy place at such times.

I discovered that a local church came in on a regular basis, and I was most impressed that the members knew every resident by name. I struggled with knowing the names of the staff, but this group knew every resident, and all the staff. The quality of their music was excellent and Adrian enjoyed the rhythm and the singing of the worship songs and hymns, many from his childhood. He was always brighter and happier after such visits.

I quickly realised that Adrian was not limited to sitting in a chair as he had been at home where he had needed help to sit down, and where I been forced to watch him twenty-four hours a day to try and keep him safe. Somehow he had found his legs and his confidence in sitting down, giving him much more freedom. In the bungalow if he moved one of the family would follow. Indeed we even installed a baby alarm to watch him when he was asleep in case he suddenly got up and needed the bathroom. There was no guarantee he would make it, and the carpet bore the brunt of this. Now though, he could walk where he wanted, sit in different lounges, watch the television or not, and engage with other residents. Somehow he had gained confidence. All this had disappeared when he had been at home in the bungalow.

Likewise of course Adrian's going into the Home gave me the freedom. I had not realised how curtailed I had been during the previous year. I had hardly left him alone for months. I was always on duty twenty-four hours a day, seven days a week, and while I sought only to care for him and keep him safe, it had almost unknowingly been a big drain upon me. Now I could give the grandchildren more attention, and in the Spring I joined D___ and the grandchildren in going to London where we visited Legoland. I felt very sad at the time for Adrian would have so enjoyed going there with the children, but reality had by now set in and I was content that he was cared for by staff that were growing very fond of him.

Having let Adrian settle into the Home before I visited, I decided to allow some time to elapse before the grandchildren went to see their grandfather. So it was early spring before the two children went to see Adrian. I was slightly concerned about taking them into the Home. Some residents had multiple problems and would shout at visitors, or suddenly scream, or make strange noises. Others would sit banging an object on a table for hours on end. I was unsure how the youngsters would cope with this and whether it would worry them. In the event when they first came in with me to see Adrian they took it all in their stride. They brought in a picture to put in his room, took photographs of him, and sat chatting with him. When the tea came round they were presented with some cake and a drink. Our granddaughter sat on a small settee with him, giving him cuddles, and he stroked her hair. She was obviously missing having him at home, and even if he was unsure who she was, he was happy to be entertained by her. Adrian was at his best. His sense of humour had come back, and he was full of witty remarks. He was obviously really pleased to see the children, and blew them both kisses as they left.

Over the next few months they would talk to the staff, pick up things dropped by the residents or help to give them their food if it were out of reach. They would reassure those who were upset, and follow Adrian around the Home. Occasionally they would go through the memory box that he had brought into the Home with him, and try to engage him in conversation, although this got much harder as time went on. At home they would ask me when they could go and see Adrian again, and always remembered to take something new in to show him. The experience was probably very character-forming for them.

At Easter both our sons returned home for the holiday. K___ and our daughter-in-law R___ had not seen the Nursing Home, and were impressed by the imposing set up. They liked the size of Adrian's room, which would have easily taken two people. We had done a lot to try and make it seem familiar to him by hanging up well-known pictures, and putting ornaments from his old flat in Gloucester on the window-sill.

However, K___ found the whole experiencing of seeing his father in the Home upsetting particularly as he felt that Adrian blamed him for being there. In fact he had not been at home when the decision had been made, but his brother D___ had, so perhaps Adrian had confused his two sons at this point. While we were visiting he had stared at K___ before pointing a very direct finger at him and saying "You!" in a loud and angry voice. It was as though he blamed him for being in the Nursing Home, yet it had been our older son who had actually taken him there because I had a diabetic eye-screen test that particular day. I felt very sad for K___, but there was nothing than any of us could do about it.

The following day when D___ went to see his father I was concerned what might happen. Like me he was impressed at the way Adrian had settled into the Home, and despite what had happened the day before Adrian reacted in a very calm way to him.

I found Easter Day a little difficult, perhaps because it was the first such festival without Adrian. I noticed that I was still counting how many weeks he had been in the Nursing Home. It took another couple of months before I stopped doing this.

PAYING FOR THE COST OF RESIDENTIAL CARE

After some weeks I was called to an Assessment Meeting to consider whether Adrian would get full nursing care payment, or whether I would be asked to pay for some of his care. Each professional Carer (the Social Worker, the Psychiatric nurse, Sue the owner of the Nursing Home, and the Manager of the Home) was asked to complete pages of information. I was also asked to fill in a large form concerning Adrian. At the end of some weeks all the professional workers came together with me to make recommendations on a scale of one to five. The highest grade was five, and if he were to receive full nursing care then he needed at least two of these. By the end of the meeting it looked as though I would receive full care, but I couldn't be sure until I heard back, officially.

It was a very nervous time as I waited to hear the result of the deliberations of a great number of people. If the answer was negative then I was going to pay a lot of money to keep Adrian in the Nursing Home. I knew I couldn't afford this. However, after a few weeks the decision was made, and I received a letter confirming that Adrian would receive full nursing care, largely because of his delusions and his unpredictability. It was possible, they concluded, that he could hurt himself or someone else. It was a considerable relief to me and to the whole family that he was to be funded, though I was warned that if the situation changed then so might funding. When I asked about this clause apparently it meant that if he became bedridden he might lose the funding, because he would no longer be a danger to others! This felt absolutely crazy!

Three months after Adrian went into the Nursing Home the first of our elderly Labrador dogs died, and two weeks later the second dog died. The children and I were devastated, but the dogs were over fourteen years old. They had been together since their birth as they were litter-mates. We decided not to tell Adrian. He had loved the dogs so much and walked them most days, but he rarely if ever talked about them now. It was possible that he would be upset if I told him, and I didn't think he needed this extra unhappiness. The Home would have welcomed us bringing in the dogs, but because of their age and frailty I had never done this. During the next year he didn't mentioned the dogs, so I never had to say that they had died. It wasn't until very near the end of his life that a question about the dogs came up.

THOSE WHO VISITED ADRIAN

After Adrian was settled in the Home I began to visit him regularly once or twice a week. I still had the grandchildren to care for and couldn't get there more often, so I asked some of our friends to go and see him. I chose those who had a natural ability to emphasise with other people, who could try to understand Adrian's world from his perspective. My closest friend, Anne, with whom we had gone on holiday the previous year was only too happy to go and visit him, at first with me and then on her own. This really helped me while I still had the children at home, and when I took on more responsibility in the parish. It meant that I was able to keep in closer contact with the Home during this time.

Adrian was always receptive to women, although he also liked the company of men. In the past he could walk into a strange pub and within one evening learn all there was to know about the village. My mother had always thought it amazing that when we went on holiday Adrian would return at the end of an evening to give her all the local information she could want. Yet if he was happy to talk to the local men at the bar, he had always enjoyed the company of women. So I found two or three women who were happy to visit him in the Home. Sometimes he would engage with them, at other times he would simply sit quietly dozing. On another visit he might laugh and joke with them. We discovered that if he was silent and two people were visiting, then he would try to join in their conversation. At that point those visiting could begin to include him and allow the talk to go in the direction he led. This proved to be a really good way of enabling Adrian to participate. If only one person visited, as soon as they spoke to a member of staff he would want join in the conversation. Those with dementia often lose the ability to give or to help others, and everyone around them is always making them the object of their care, so being able to participate in a conversation is an important skill for them to retain. It was good to see Adrian attempting to join in what was happening around him.

I noticed that in the relaxed atmosphere of the Home, residents were still able to offer help to one another. Those with less advanced dementia were often seen working together, and caring for the less able. This wasn't always helpfully received, but it was lovely to see, and was encouraged by the staff. Tables and chairs would be removed if they were perceived as being in the way, or given to other residents who needed somewhere to put a cup of tea. Cushions would be offered to someone who seemed to need one, and items picked up of the floor when they had accidentally been dropped. Visitors also engaged in this. Our granddaughter helped one elderly resident by picking up the doll the latter had been holding. This finally turned into a hilarious game, with the doll being dropped and retrieved until both were exhausted.

In the Summer I took a Hand-Bell Group into the Home. The response of the residents to any kind of music was always well received. The group were fairly new and none of us were sure if we'd be able to play the pieces all the way through, or whether the tune would collapse. However, the seven or eight bell-ringers that day managed to play the old English songs very well, and the residents who had all been gathered into the large lounge obviously enjoyed the music. While we were waiting for tea one of the group started to sing and the rest of us joined her. It was noticeable that a few of the residents joined in, one in Welsh. Since all our music had been of the 'Bobby Shafto' and 'Clementine' variety, most of those present would have learnt these as children at school, as I had. They knew most of the words and some enjoyed singing or humming the old songs with us.

Over tea the members of the group took the bells round for residents to play them, and I was pleased to see that they engaged in repetition and mimicry to encourage participation. Rather than just giving them a hand-bell they showed them what to do before handing the bell over for the resident to copy. Whatever the result it was greeted with big smiles and claps, and they were encouraged to try again. Everyone was intrigued by the small coloured bells and their clear tone. One or two rang them vigorously thoroughly pleased at the sound, even though by now the room had erupted in a cacophony of noise. Unfortunately Adrian was given a yellow bell and once he was encouraged to hold the bell he promptly turned it upside down and tried to eat it. He obviously thought it was an ice-cream. I was reminded again that what we think is needed for someone with dementia is not necessarily what they think is needed.

The behaviour of many people with dementia is often a result of that meted out to them. Frowns or irritation will often be met by stubbornness or even anger, and smiles and laughter by one of pleasure. Perhaps the old proverb 'As you sow, so shall you reap' is particularly appropriate. Another way of putting it is to say that dementia sufferers are not often proactive, but are more often than not reactive. The happy, laughing faces around me that afternoon seemed to prove the old adage to be true as they responded to the joyful sound of music and to the smiling, encouraging faces around them in the room.

BIRTHDAY CELEBRATIONS

On the 4th of July we celebrated Adrian's seventy-fourth birthday with a beautiful cake made by the cook in the Home, and with lots of balloons and a number of presents. Anne and some of the other people who visited Adrian came in to join me and helped make it a special day for him. Adrian seemed to know what we were doing, certainly he clapped when we all sang 'Happy birthday' to him, but he might have assumed the celebration was for someone else. Visitors helped him to open the presents, but he showed little interest in them, except for one.

This was a toy dalmatian dog. As it appeared from the wrapping paper his face lit up, and he exclaimed. "Oggie Doggie!" His memory had gone back to forty-six years earlier when we had owned a deaf dalmatian dog before either of our two boys were born. She was a completely mad albino bitch, with no spots on her face, but with one blue eye and one with a black spot over the pupil. Adrian had loved the dog, telling everyone about her escapades - how she would escape but because she was deaf how hard it was to get her back. She would turn and see us, and then deliberately run in the opposite direction.

In Norfolk she would constantly find a way out of the back garden and Adrian would get a phone call from the Station Commander's office, saying "Your xxxx dog is on my airfield! Get it off!" Since it was a working airfield with RAF planes taking off and landing it was amazing she (or the C.O.!) survived.

Adrian would tell the people in the pub at night that "She understands everything I say!" In fact he would indicate to her through signals with his hands, point down to sit, or to the door to say they were leaving. All went well until she met someone with a 'wall eye', and she would sit and bark solidly at him, presumably because she thought he was staring at her.

Oggie almost died one year during the time that England was suffering a series of electricity strikes. We both went out that morning – Adrian to work, and myself to College. The electricity had gone off while we were getting breakfast, but we thought nothing of it. Amazingly that particular day Adrian had a phone call to say a man was coming to do some work on the house, so he popped back in his coffee break to let him into the place. Opening the kitchen door he found the entire room blanketed in thick black smoke, and Oggie lying on the floor with her nose pressed to the air hole at the bottom of the pantry. When the electricity had returned the toaster had come on, but the bread had curled up and kept on burning. Luckily Oggie was alright, although she was terrified of any coal fire and of shadows for evermore.

It was Oggie that had gone to the Isle of Man with us when we took a choir of thirty teenagers from the church choir on a singing holiday. Sleeping in a hall we would let Oggie out to run over all the camp beds – it was the quickest way to get the teenagers out of bed! All the youngsters would take her out for walks, and there was only one day after going for about fifty 'walks' that she refused to leave the hall. When the last couple of children dangled the lead in front of her face, she looked sorrowfully at them and lay down on a camp bed, exhausted.

Unfortunately she was run over a few weeks before our son D___ was born, but Adrian had never forgotten Oggie. In his confused mind, when he was unable to remember virtually anything, he was able to go back immediately to our first dog who had made a huge impact upon him. The memory was still bright and clear in his mind, and because of this the toy dog had a very special place in his room, although whether he remembered the incidents concerning Oggie I never quite knew.

On the day of his birthday he had been given a fair few boxes of sweets and chocolates, and well as toiletries. Months later I was to find all of these unused in his room, along with the unopened Easter eggs. No-one had thought to open them for him, and I was to blame as much as the staff, so they just sat in a drawer unused and uneaten.

I realised it was really better to buy him clothes. As his body shape shrunk I constantly had to buy him new clothes. It meant at times like Christmas and his birthday that I could spend a little more on them. I resisted buying jogging trousers or track-suits. He would never have worn them before the dementia. After twenty-two years in the RAF he was accustomed to wearing a shirt and collar, and was always happy in a suit. I compromised now with shirts, jumpers, and grey or dark blue trousers but no ties. He looked a little less lost, and a little more like the Adrian we had all known for years.

Adrian's general health over the past few years had been reasonably good. He had undergone a period of depression the previous year, which was understandable. He was prescribed some medicine, but it didn't suit him, and he quickly came off the tablets. After that he managed without any help. The only other thing that had caused him problems concerned his blood pressure, which in 2012 was very high for a while. This was to happen again some time later.

Two days after his birthday, the Doctor was called into the Home to see Adrian. His blood pressure was up again and it looked as though he had had a small TIA (transient ischaemic attack) or mini-stroke. There was a slight weakness on the right-side of his body, and a list to one side when he walked. After a few days it got better, but I thought he looked much frailer and older than he had been. As we ended the summer, friends who visited during the holidays along with my brother and his wife, certainly noticed the changes in him.

FIFTIETH WEDDING ANNIVERSARY

A much larger celebration was held on 11th September on our fiftieth wedding anniversary. Although we had rarely done anything special on our anniversary and didn't give each other anything, this was a very special occasion and I did want to spend some time with him. To my utter amazement the entrance porch of the Home had balloons and banners and a picture of both Adrian and I to celebrate the day. All the corridors had gas-filled balloons and banners festooned everywhere. I was invited into the main lounge where everyone was waiting for both of us and a huge cake was brought in. It was a really wonderful party. The only sad thing was to see Adrian sitting there looking totally bemused, with absolutely no awareness of the importance of the day, and completely unaware that we were even married.

I had the foresight to think ahead, and since I hadn't wanted to spend the evening at home on my own (feeling sorry for myself) I had decided to hold a dinner party for ten people at home. It was a wonderful way to end such a special day.

A NEW GRANDSON

In November our daughter-in-law R___ gave birth to a beautiful baby boy on Guy Fawkes day. I did tell Adrian upon my return from the Midlands and showed him pictures of the new baby, but the information meant nothing to him. I wasn't sure if he even knew he was looking at the picture of a baby. I did mention him every time I went in to the Home, for he so loved babies and young children and would have enjoyed welcoming another baby into the family.

CHRISTMAS AND THE NEW YEAR

Christmas was quiet, since all of us missed Adrian's presence. I was working hard, as the Vicar had been off work on long-term sickness since the autumn, and I took the Midnight Service at the parish church. For me it was simply not the same without Adrian in the congregation, and knowing that this is how it would always be from now on was not a pleasant thought.

In February Anne and I were able to go to Israel with a Diocesan Pilgrimage group, which was a wonderful opportunity. I was sad that I was going without Adrian, although we had both gone to the Holy Land together in the past. The most difficult day occurred when we went to Cana in Galilee, to the church built over the place where Jesus was supposed to have carried out the miracle of turning water into wine at a wedding ceremony. As we went into the church there were a large number of elderly Japanese or Korean couples celebrating their fiftieth wedding anniversaries. Having recently celebrated our fiftieth anniversary I was unable to go into the church, for the memory of Adrian in a Nursing Home was simply too poignant for a few moments.

THE LAST NINE MONTHS

Over the next nine months vascular dementia ravaged Adrian's body. Sometimes I would visit and there would be no visible sign that he knew I was present. At other

176

times I would get a smile or a final wave. Occasionally he would say odd words or sentences, which led me to believe that he thought he was at work controlling the computer. One night Sue found him wandering the corridors still talking about work, and she stopped and talked with him.

Adrian had never been fond of sweet food, preferring savoury things, and as a diabetic it had suited him not to eat them. His sugar levels were always good because of this. But now with the constant battle to keep his weight from dropping off he was eating cakes, puddings, and chocolate. I would take him a bar of chocolate every time I went to visit, and he would happily eat half of it, even when he wasn't acknowledging my presence. It was amazing to see what a sweet tooth he now had.

Sometimes I would read to him, or even sing to him and to others in the room. If I ran out of words, I would make them up, and then promptly repeat them or even resort to "la-la-ing". It was the sound of a voice, whether speaking or singing, that appealed to the residents, not necessarily the words. One visitor who came in to the Home regularly played a small accordion, and I began to sing to accompany the traditional songs that she was playing. From the tapping feet and fingers, and the occasional words from a person that joined in I think it was appreciated.

As the dementia grew worse Adrian would only respond to large scale gestures from those around him. One of the Carers was always able to get a response from him. She would put her head round the door and with a loud voice ask him for a kiss, before blowing one to him. He would always smile and laugh at her while ignoring those around him who were too timid to show more grandiose gestures. This continued right up until his death. At other times if there was silence around him he would often glance at his visitors out of the corner of his eye, but when they looked at him he would look away.

All of his family and friends had been shocked as I said, by the screams and shouts that would emanate from his room when anyone was trying to clean or dress him. During the last two months of his life when Adrian was still being particularly difficult about dressing in the morning one new member of staff asked me if we had ever had any dogs. Apparently when he was refusing to let people put his socks and shoes on in the morning she understood him to say "dog" at some point, and then later the word "beach". She asked me if Adrian had ever had a dog, and if he had ever walked it on the beach. When I told her that we'd had two chocolate Labradors but that they had since died, and that in the past he frequently took them down to the beach, she said she had an idea that might help Adrian to get dressed in the morning.

A few days later the same Carer came to me to tell me what had happened when she and another member of staff were helping Adrian to get dressed the following morning. He showed his usual unhappiness and tried to stop them putting on his trousers, and his socks and shoes.

At that point she said, "Come on, the dogs need their walk on the beach!"

After that every time he hesitated, she reminded him that he was going down to the beach to walk the dogs that were waiting for him. Apparently he was completely happy to finish getting dressed, and a few minutes later he was ready for his breakfast. This episode happened nearly twenty months after Adrian had last seen the two dogs, yet mention of them sparked in his damaged brain something that made sense for that moment.

Not long after this though a member of staff said "He's now too compliant!" and I knew what he meant. The fight had gone out of him. He was too sick to care whether or not anyone wanted to dress him or clean him.

One of the things that did impress me throughout these twenty months was that despite Adrian's constant fight with the staff, when at least three of them had to deal with him, it never affected their patience or compassion. They would still call him a "gentleman". When this fight stopped everyone was saddened, because somehow it wasn't Adrian. We knew it wouldn't be long to go now.

Family and friends who came in the last months of his life were all shocked by the change in Adrian. Some refused to see him, preferring as they said "to remember him as he was". I found this very difficult, for it felt as though I was even more isolated. It was impossible for me to talk with those who didn't know the reality of his life, and I found their attitude selfish. They seemed to have no concept that Adrian might have needed visitors, or that it would take some of the burden from those of us who went in week in and week out. Some of those who didn't wish to go into the Home were, I think afraid of being upset, and although I understood this it was very hurtful that they were unable to go and visit him.

I was so proud of our sons who always made sure they visited their father when they were in Pembrokeshire. Both of them lived a long way from Wales, yet made time to come and see me and their father. My brother and his wife from Southsea, both visited Adrian and I am sure were saddened knowing that it was the last time they would see him, but I was grateful for their support. Jane our friend from Worcester, never failed to visit Adrian and it meant that I could talk with her about him, and then of course there was Anne and the little group of ladies from the village who continually visited him in the Home.

Towards the end of July K___ and his wife R___ came to stay for a few days, and took their eight month baby son to see Adrian. Although they got little response he did make an effort to look at him and wave his fingers in front of the baby's face, but this was really the last time he made such an effort for a child. By mid-August I was visiting Adrian every other day as his health deteriorated. The Doctor or Surgery Nurse and the on-duty Nurse in the Home frequently visited him during this time, but there was little anyone could do and it was obvious that he was slowly coming to the end of his life.

D___ saw him on his way back to Suffolk, and then on the twenty-fourth of September he became very ill and I was forced to email both sons that they should come and see him as soon as possible. D___ is a teacher, and was running weekend courses and was unable to get back, but K___ came to say goodbye to his father three days later. He found him comfortable and in minimal pain and before he left Adrian made eye contact with him and nodded. To me it felt like a benediction.

I visited every other day after this, and the night before he died in October Anne and I saw Adrian. He had been virtually bed-bound for some weeks, but this afternoon he was in the large living room in a chair. We prayed with him and I kissed him goodbye. He died peacefully that night, and I was so very glad to have seen him the day before.

14. ADRIAN'S DEATH AND AFTER-WARDS

My first response on being told of Adrian's death was absolute relief. He had suffered much in the last few years and particularly in the previous six months. Although he had been comfortable at the Nursing Home and very well-looked after, his quality of life recently had been very poor. The only thing that cheered me up during this time was that he seemed unaware of anything, other than pain, and this had been managed as best as they could by the Carers at the Home. However, one could not wish such a life for anyone, and now that it was over I felt total relief.

I also acknowledged that I had begun to say my goodbyes to Adrian nearly three years before, and in particular when he had left our home to enter the Nursing Home. He hadn't known who I was for some years, and although this didn't matter because I knew he was my husband, nevertheless the ties between us had already begun to loosen. This was accelerated when I would return home to an empty bungalow after the grandchildren returned to their mother in Peru, with no children, no dogs and no grandchildren in the place. Always one of the most difficult things about losing someone is facing the empty home, and I had already coped with that, and had begun to learn how to look after myself without the help of a much loved partner.

Another aspect of bereavement is the inability to tell a loved one what has happened during the day – to share the interesting memories - and this had already been faced long before Adrian's death. K___ told me that he felt the same; the pain over the death of his father had been spread over the previous two years. Both of us may well have seemed somewhat callous to other people, but it was a fact that we were a long way down the bereavement path. The lovely father and husband that we knew so well had left us a very long time ago.

Now I lived with my memories of a wonderfully kind man, who was my rock, and without whom I would never have had the kind of life I had experienced. Because of him I went to University, and because of him I became a priest. In some ways he was a man ahead of his time, and was content to live a peaceful existence helping those he could whether it be fostering a teenager, taking on a deaf dalmatian, or giving a home to his grandchildren, all of which he had done during his life. He was unassuming, compassionate, and a true British gentleman with a great sense of humour, and will be much missed.

FROM THE AUTHOR

Copies of this book can be ordered from:
lulu.com
Amazon.co.uk

HELP

For those living in the UK who might need help concerning the whole subject of dementia, they can do no better than ring the **National Dementia Helpline**: 0300 222 11 22 or contact their online community.

Alternatively contact **Dementia UK** on 0800 888 6678.

****

NOTE:

Sharon Swain also writes novels under her maiden name: Sharon Collier:

Escape to Silent Valley
The Dying River
The Eighth Day

Printed in Great Britain
by Amazon